Thomas Minor

Diary Of Thomas Minor, Stonington Connecticut, 1653 to 1684

Thomas Minor

Diary Of Thomas Minor, Stonington Connecticut, 1653 to 1684

ISBN/EAN: 9783337185183

Printed in Europe, USA, Canada, Australia, Japan

Cover: Foto ©ninafisch / pixelio.de

More available books at **www.hansebooks.com**

THE DIARY

OF

THOMAS MINOR,

STONINGTON, CONNECTICUT.

1653 to 1684.

Prepared for publication by SIDNEY H. MINER
and GEORGE D. STANTON, JR.

1899.

INTRODUCTION.

This Diary was undertaken by Thomas Minor for the double purpose of refreshing his own memory concerning current events, and for the use of his immediate family. It is at least plausible that because of his partial isolation in the wilds of the New England Colony the consecutive entries of dates were made by him also for the purpose of a record of time, for it will be remembered that at that period of our history calendars were not usually found among the inhabitants, and there was a considerable sameness of the passage of days from one to another.

He has said that it was not his purpose that the Diary go beyond the use of his immediate family, but considering the age of the writing and the various matters contained in the Diary, interesting from the point of knowing how the earliest settlers lived at home and treated the events of importance to themselves and family, and its value to those searching for missing record entries, it has been considered advisable to perpetuate the Diary by printing it, following the orthography and punctuation strictly and the contents generally in every particular.

The legibility of the writing is fast becoming obscured aided by the mutilation of the paper from age, and it has been only possible to translate it now by the aid of a powerful magnifying glass in places, while some of it is wholly illegible.

The Diary has been handed down through successive generations remaining on the old Thomas Minor homestead property at Quiambaug, in the town of Stonington, Conn., and is now in the custody of Cornelius V. Miner.

The writer of the Diary, Thomas Minor, came from Somersett County, England, on the good ship Arabella, which landed at Salem, Massachusetts, the 14th day of June, 1630. His sterling qualities placed him in the position to at once become a prominent figure in the affairs of the Colony. He early allied himself with the men of authority and soon became recognized in their Councils for his sound judgment. He was a recognized authority in dealing with the Indians, and because of his peculiar ability to deal with them was frequently employed by Governor Winthrop to enter into agreements with, and publish court orders to the tribes.

It is said that he mastered the language and on occasions would accompany a missionary as interpreter to give them the gospel in their own language. We also find him leading the militia against the

Narragansett Indians, and at an age when man's qualifications as a leader of soldiers are not considered worth anything.

He seems to have taken particular pride in entering in the Diary the numerous occasions when "Mr. Winthrop" was his guest, and many times the two are recorded as meeting at the old Mill and other places and talking over the topics of interest.

Between the years 1630 and 1640 Thomas Minor lived at Salem, Charlestown, and Hingham, Mass., but he was not satisfied to settle down in any of those places, and we find a commission of the General Court of Massachusetts, that "Whereas, Mr. John Winthrop Jr. and others have by allowance of this Court begun a plantation in the Pequot Colony which appertains to this jurisdiction as part of our proportion to the conquered country, we grant, etc.," to Mr. Winthrop, Thomas Peters, Thomas Minor, Isaac Wiley, Cary Latham, Jacob Westerhouse, William Morton, John Stebbins and others. Under this commission we find Thomas Minor one of the founders of what he is pleased to call "Pequit," now New London, and here for a while he makes it his home. But it is after he has determined to settle permanently at "Quiambaug," on lands which he has acquired partly by grant, because of valuable services with the Indians, during the year 1653 or 1654 that he takes up the

Diary and carries it on faithfully till July 26th, 1684.

The wild character of the country about his place may be seen from his frequent references to the loss of stock by wolves, and the killing of deer. Indians were frequent visitors and often sought employment from him, payment being made in clothes.

Associating himself with others the town of South-erton, (sometimes called by him Southerntown) now Stonington, was formed in 1600. Referring to the numerous offices held by him from time to time we find a partial list in the following entry in the Diary:

"I was by the Town and this year chosen to be a select man the Town treasurer the towns recorder The brander of horses by the general Court Recorded the head officer of the Train band by the same Court one of the ffour that have the charge of the milishcia of the whole Countie and chossen and sworn Commissionor and one to assist in keeping the Countie Courte."

In the life of Thomas Minor we have a prominent example of those men, who with their families, came to this country and fulfilled the purpose of time in creating in the new world a people of illimitable resources, jealous of personal rights, with brawny arms and fertile brain and with the unconquerable perseverance so characteristic of the pioneer settlers who attacked the forces of nature's wilderness that a nation might be built for the world to respect.

THE THOMAS MINOR DIARY.

After the leape y
2: of our lord god
the Creation & the th
(Worn off) After the leape yeare   (Worn off)
care 1663 of our lord god in the
yeare and from the Creation
yeare : 5612
yeare 1664 : of our lord god is
first year after the leap
year and from the creation 5613.

New Commiss
(Worn off)   & all other offic   (Worn off)
the whole compa
Met it was agreed that
day namely the : 28 : of No
every year all the officers
chosen for the time to co   e
that time Mr. Thomas Stanton
Chosen Commissioner

(1653-4) (The) ninth month november   (torn) tusday the first wensday the 2. it snowed and thursday the .3. it rained and tusday the .8. was at mill. the wensday being the (torn) was a day of thanksgiving and tusday the .15. I gathered turneps (and) pasneps and tusday .22. I was about fensing of my hay at Poquatucke and tusday the .29. John cam home and it was a storm & wensday the .30.

the .2. of December Mr. Haynes his cattel was delivered unto me being friday

The tenth month desember .31. days thursday the first, thursday the .8. and wensday the .14. Captin masons man Came for one yoke of oxen and thursday the .15. & thursday the .22. I had plowed two days crose the (la)nd and this same day I begun to (torn) timber at the mill broocke We-(que-te-quoc) (torn) the .29. I plowed a littell and friday the .30. it rained and I (torn) 500 of pales Clover and (torn) day my Brothors brought (torn) from Poquatucke and (torn) .31.

(The) Eleventh month Januarie .31 (days saba)th day the first (mo)nday (torn) (deliver)ed .2. oxen to Aron Starke for the yuse of major masson satterday the (torn) theare was a greate snow sabat day (torn) monday the .9. we fetched the mare I could not find the swine & sabath day .15. ther was aded another

great snow the (torn) came whome thursday the .19.
the snow all melted & friday .20. I made an end
Cleaving of pals at the mill br(ooke) ther was aleven
hundred pals and sabath day the .22. the 26. and 27
I (torn) sabath day the 29. tusday the

The twelvth month februarie .28. days the second
yeare after the leape yeare wensday the first and
monday the (6) made an end of cross plowing and
wensday the .8. I had 9 peeces to hew .3. seventeen
foot (torn) 14 foot loung 9 ynches and .6. the (same)
day I looked for the mare wensday the 15. thursday
the 16 I came from (Conet)icut & wensday the .22.
it was (ver)ie darke storme and did snow (tus)day
.28. I fetched the catell (Poqu)atuck.

The last will of Thomas Minor m(ade) the .8. of
februarie 1653: if I die or com no more I doe bequeath and give all that I have house and lands goods
and cattell To my wife grace minor and do leave the
whole disposing of my children to her for any debts
that I ow to be paid by her and then the rest to be
hers for her owne maintainance and our Childrens
and this do I witness by setting To my hand the .8.
of februariè 1653.   Thomas Minor

Thursday the .2. of march gentill calved monday
the 13 brown calved and wensday the .15. kent
calved.   (Cipher)

Satterday the .11. of Aprill. 1657. sonnamoot brought .2. quarts and one pinte of lickquor to our house and said he gave 10s. for it a(t) goodman shaw and yt his wife gave it him.

The first month is march .1654 and hath .31 days wensday the first friday the third John went to Coneticut & tusday the .7. I made an End of hewing of timber at the mill brooke watch came backe from Coneticut and wensday the eight I begun to plow the wheat land and monday the .13. I made an End of sowing of wheate and wensday the .15. I made an End of sowing pasnepes and monday the .22. I looked for the swine and wensday .29. I vewed Cary lathams farm and friday .31

The second month is Aprile and hath .30. days satterday the first and satterday the .8. and monday the .10. I begun at the farme at Mistuksuck and satterday the .15. monday the .17. I began to plant and satturday the .22 wainpeter caried coren to mill the .24. day being monday I made an End of planting of Indean Corne and satterday the .29 and sabath day the .30.

Sabiantwosucke promised the .30. of desember befor mr stanton and tomus shaw to make Watch a

Facsimile of will and cipher in Diary.   (See page 7).

canoow for that which I had and to bring me six pecks of nunip (Indian word for beans.)

The third month is may .31. days monday the first sabath day being the .7. my Brothers came with the Cattell and monday the .8. and wensday the .10. I received .2. oxen (eighteen pounds) and one cow (and six pounds) of my father-in(law) and one sheer and Culter and monday the .15 and monday the .22. ffathers Calfes wer driven to our farme and it rained that day and monday the 29 and wensday the .31.
                    (Cipher)

The fourth month is June .30. days thursday the first and thursday the .8. day and sabath day the .11. (omitted) and thursday the .15. I went to Coneticut & thursday .22. John came whome and satterday .24. I made an end of carrying of timber & Thursday .29. friday the .30.

received from Conecticut one paier of boots 10 and one paier of shews .11. one paier .10.one paier .7. two paier of 9 one paier for Samuel and one paier of ould John had,

The fiffe month is July .31. days satterday the first I had mowed 3 days at mistick and satterday the 8 and saterday the .15. I made two reeps at the ffarme and satterday the .22. I had reaped my Rie and oats and one acker of wheate my father was gone to seaconcke and satterday .29. monday 31.

The sixt month is agust .31. days tusday the first wensday the .2. I had set up the wheate at mistuksset and it rained and tusday the .8. I made an end threshing and paid mother the .2. bushels of Rie and tusday the .15. I made an End of making of hay at the farme and tusday the .22. the day before I begun to frame at mistuckeset & tusday the .29. thursday 31.

The seventh month is september .30. days friday the first and friday the .8. I had lost the cattell at Mistucksset and tusday the 12 twelth I begun to gather coren and friday the .15. and friday the .22. we had two hundred shocks and fouer made at the farme of Indean Coren & one hundred and fortie and friday the 29. I made an end of shockin. coren it was micaelmas day and saterday the 30. we may if we will.

The eight month is october .31. days sabath day the first and sabath day the .8. I had raised the baren and sabath day the .15. the greate storme was and I had newly raised my roofe of my house and thursday the .19. I sowed the winter wheate and sabath day the .22. and sabath day 29 and monday the .30. I went to Coneticut tusday .31

The ninth month is november .30. days wensday the first John begun his time with mr. Stone and wensday the .8. I was at Pequit and wensday the .15 goodman redfild was making our backe for our Chimbloy and wensday the .22. our backe of our Chimbly was ended goodman Redfild had 22s & 6d for doing the stone walle monday the 27th I made an end of planting of trees & tusday .28. Thomas Stanton tooke Mr fitches .2. cattell to winter and wensday the .29. we threshed our indean corne and thursday the .30

The tenth month is december .31. days friday the first and friday the .8. I threshed wheat and had ten bushells and friday the .15. I fetched whome stones and made the hearth I had threshed rie but not winnowed I had .15. bushels and friday the .22. I made an end of threshing I had .5. bushells of oats and monday .25. it was Chrismas day and friday .29. sabath day the .31. day

I had made an end with Watch about his canoow at Mr stantons.

The eleventh month is Januarie .31. days monday the first and is called new year day sabath day the .7. I was at Pequit river and could not get over and monday the eight and monday the .15. ther was a verie great snow fell and monday the .22. the snow melted all away tusday .23. I was at mill and monday .29. tusday .30. Brown Calved wensday the .31.

thursday the .8. of februarie Captain Denison tould me that he was with Robert hempstead and I when we laid out major masson his land and that he well did remember all the marked trees and that it was to run to but the head of the salt cove.

The twelvth month is februarie .28. days and the third yeare after the leap yeare thursday the first and thursday the .8. we drseed the sumer hemp and thursday the .15. I made an end of hewing of planks for the house and thursday the .22. and wensday the .23. the 5 yeare.

The .5. of march .1654. I gave Captine denison a list of what I had fower oxen five cows fower yarlings and ten ackers of land buting upon the river at pequit and the farme that I bought of Cary latham by me   Thomas Minor.

The .28. of Agust being monday I was sent for to pequit for to be reconsiled to the Church and at evening the maigor pt met at goodman Calkins hous namly Mr. Blinman Mr. Bruen Goodman calkin Ralph perker goodman Lester goodman Morgan goodman coit hugh Roberts Captain denison and goodman Cheesbrough being there all there tooke satisfaction in my acknowledging the height of my spirit Secondly in that I saw my evill in my suden and rash speaking to Mr Blinman and with all ther was acknowledment on the Churches pt that I was wronged so all was passed by on my side and the Churches with pmise on both p'ties that all formor offences should be buried and never more to be agitateed so desiring the praiers each for other we pted form that meeting Agust .28. 1654.

The first month is march and hath .31. days being the yeare 1655. Thursday the first and thursday the eight I went to mill and thursday the .15. that weeke I had Arons oxen to plow and thursday .22. I was at mill goodman Lester was married
sabath day .25. and our lady day as it is so called monday the .26. the major had a letter read in a towne meeting of which he desired an ackor of land and an Iland thursday .29. and satterday the .31. I raised the frame of my Chimbly.

The secone month is Aprile and hath .30. days sabath day the first and thursday the .5. I made an End of covering the house and friday the .6. I sowed wheate and satterday the .7. I begun to garden and sabath day the .8. and sabath day the .15. I was at Coneticut and came whome on thursday being the

.19. the .13. of this month being friday John began to board with the widow Smith and sabath day the .22. monday .23. I made and end of gardning tusday .24. I sowed hemp and sabath day .29. monday the .30.

The third month is may and hath .31. days tusday the first and tusday the .8. and tusday the .15. maijor mason had sent a second letter to the townsmen about the land I delivered the fourtie ackers of land to goodman Keeny for the five ackers of meadow I had of him and tusday the .22. I bought the new canoow and tusday the .29. and thursday the .31.

The .2. of June being Satterday John came whome, and brought a Canoow and Coopers vesels the canoow cost .20. shillings the new one .23. shillings and 6 pence.

The fourth month is June and hath .30. days friday the first and satterday the .2. we had the wooll from goodwife shaw and tusday the .5. I had a calfe of Aron Starke in parte of pay for my hat and 9 shillings still is due and friday the .8. the Indeans begun to play and friday the .15. I begun to weed upon the plaine at this time the Court was at pequit and friday the .22. and friday the .29. I made an end of weeding and did the hedg by the waters side Satterday the .30.

The fift month is July and hath .31. days sabath day the first and Sabath day the .8. we had a sacrament and sabath day 15 monday the 16 the lists were to be brought in and wer finished about the Contrie rate and mr Blinman and the Towne rate and sabath day the .22. I had hilled halfe the new ground and puld the sumer hemp and thursday .26. John was heare and satterday the 28 I made an end of Cuting sumer wheate sabath day .29. tusday 31.

The sixt month is Agust and hath .31. days wensday the first and wensday the .8. I sould the Bark to picket and borrowed halfe one bushell of salt of goodman Kenny and wensday the .15. and wensday the .22. and wensday the .29. friday .31.

The seventh month is september and hath .30. days satterday the first and satterday the .8. Clement went to pequit alone wensday the .12. I made an end of sowing of winter wheate and satterday the .15. my wife was delivered of hana and satterday the .22. and satterday the .29 and mickelmas day and sabath day the .30.

the .2. of Januarie 1656 the farme was measured by Jams Morgan and mr Brewin that I bought of Carie latham 252 akers one mile lounge & 40 pole loung.

The .8. month is october and hath .31. days monday the .1. I was to goe into the bay and monday the .22. the steer that is Caled Kent was delivered to my father palmer for deacon perke the same day John and Clement was at mill and monday the .29. wensday .31. sabath day the .28. of october hanah was baptised.

The .9. month is November and hath .30. days thursday the first and thursday the .8. I was hedging the orchard and thursday the .15. John begun his time with Captaine Culick and to be with him till the Comissioners Court next apointed at plimoth satterday the .17. the first snow fell and thursday the .22. we had kiled the white sow and gathered pasneps monday the .26. the second snow fell and thursday the .29. & friday the .30. I did the funill of the Chimbly. And Samuel Cheesbrough was married.

The tenth month is december and hath .31. days satterday the first monday the .3. I received .7. catell of deacon parke for to winter and satterday the .8. sabath day the .9. (that came from me) and satterday the .15. and satterday the .22. I fetched the littell Reecke of hay tusday the .25. and Christmas day and satterday the .29. monday the .31. I clove stufe for the barren.

The .14. of July 1657 I paid .2. pecks of winter wheate to Mr. Blinman butter 54 1£ 15s all

the .11. month is Januarie and hath .31. days tusday the first and tusday the .8. and tusday the .15. and wensday the .16. our farme was laid out at tagwouncke it lys eight score pole by goodman Cheesbroughs land the path being the south bounds from an oke at the west north west to a beech tree at the est south est and from yt by marked trees on the est side to an ashe by a spring on the north north est and from that on the north to an oke on the west north west and from that on the west to the first oke and tusday the .22. and tusday .29. thursday 31.

the .12. month is februarie and hath .29. days being the leap yeare and the yeare .1655 friday the first and friday the .8. we made an end of the barens floore and friday the .15. we Raised the barnes Roofe and friday the 22 I was at pequit and monday .25. the towne meetting was and tusday I came whome and friday the .29. being the last day of this leape yeare.

thursday being the .28. of februarie the sow piged.

1656

the first month is march and hath .31. days being the yeare .1656. and the first yeare after the leap

yeare and satterday the first I begun to thatch the
barne and satterday the .8. I made an End of clean-
ing of clapbord at Towne and satterday the .15. I
was to go to Towne with the lists and Satterday the
.22. I paid the Contrie Rate to William hough 12 s
3 d and tusday the .25. caled our lady day I had
garned one day and satterday the .29. my Brother
Sloan was heare and the major was heare and monday the .31.

The second month is Aprill and hath .30. days
Tusday the first and tusday the .8. I had begun to
plow for to plant Indean Corne and tusday the .15.
Thomas came whome and tusday the same day I
made even with Mr. Brewin and paid him all that
was his due for writting and measuring of lands tusday the .22. I had delivered pickets Cow and Calfe
to goodman sha(w) and made an end of sowing of flax
seed and pease and tusday .29. Thomas threshed
wheate and I drove the Catell to Tagwonuck there was
cheesbrough boy with .57. cattell and said that they
had .7. more at whome that is .64. he keept them 2
days going there and wensday the .30.

The third month is May and hath 31 days Thursday the first and thursday the .8. I threshed wheate
friday I fetched the Calves from loungdons and am
to keep the one for the other till may next and thurs-

day the .15. I was at mill and came safe whome the same day was the Court of Electtion at hartford and thursday the .22. I was at mill goodman Cakin came from Courte and the same day I paid Mr Blinman one firkin of butter and .12.d in wampum which made his whole years pay and thursday the .29. satterday the .31. John came from Mr Cullick about a weeke in may.

The fourth month is June and hath .30. days sabath day the first and sabath day the .8. and tusday the .10. I was to goe to bostowne with the "Lord and Erle" and sabath day the .15. and sabath day .22. I was com whome and sabath day the .29. Mr Blinman was com from Coneticut monday the .30. I had almost done mowing of the first Reeks of hay.

The .25. of this month being thursday my ffather and Cap denison was heare to veiw the fences.

The fifth month is July and hath .31. days Tusday the first and tusday the .8. we had a day of humiliation and wensday the .9. I reaped winter wheate and tusday the .15. wensday the .16. we were to measur goodman Cheesbroughs land and tusday the .22. I sowed the second sowing of turneps the .25. being fryday I set up the second hay reecke goodwife grover was heare about the boat going to the westward and Cheesbroughs talking of us and tusday .29. thursday .31.

The sixth month is Agust and hath .31. days friday the first and friday the .8. I fetched whome the mare from out of the woods and tusday the 12th. I brought whome the sheepe I did desier leave of to buy wine at the ornaries and friday the .15. I broke my sith and friday the .22. I begun my Jorney into the bay and friday the .29. I caried my chest aboard peeter Brawly his vessel at bostown sabath day the .31. tusday the .2. of september I came whome.

The seventh month is september and hath .30 days monday the first tusday the .2. I came out of the bay and monday the .8. and monday the .15. I was at pequit and monday the .22. and monday the .29. I was at the p'fecting of the list tusday the 30 we came whome from pequit from about the lists.

The eight month is october and hath .31. days wensday the first I begun to sew wheate satterday the 4 I made an end of sowi(n)g of wheat wensday the eight I made an end of mowing and wensday the .15. we were daubing the house and it was frostie weather and sabath day the .19. Captaine denison taught and wensday the .22. I was going to mill Thomas brought whome the Canoow that John found and wensday the

.29. was a day of thanksgiving friday the .31. thursday the .30. I killed the swine.

The ninth month is november and hath .30. days satterday the first and satterday the .8. we had gathered our turneps and tusday we were at the meeting at Towne about Captaine Denison being the .11. and thursday the 13 I came whome and we borrowed grovers blacke rame and begun our hedge at the yard and satterday the .15. tusday the .18. day we had threshed of winter wheate .12. bushels and satterday the .22. I made an end of the sheepe yard and satterday the .29. John had killed a deere it was the first snow sabath day the .30. wensday the .26. Ephraim was hurt with the Cart.

The tenth month is desember and hath .31. Days monday the first and wensday the .3. I went to new haven and monday the .8. and wensday the .10. I came from new haven and monday the .15. our folke wer at mill and satterday the .20. mr Tomson came to Misticke and monday the .22. and thursday the .25. and Christmas day. tusday the .23. there came an Indean Called Womponege as he said with a wen upon his right hand wrest and his left hand had upon the fore finger and the greate finger of the same 2 blue streaks of eache a bottell of lichuor as he said from Thomas Stanton and monday .29. wensday the .31.

The eleventh month is Januarie and hath .31. days thursday the first we had laid out father's land at tagwoung and thursday the .8. I was at Towne and thursday the .15. I was at Towne the day after the fast when we met about Captaine denison and other recommended Bretheren and sistors and the letters came from mr Blackman and mr fitch and thursday .22. we had fetched up the top of the stalke Reeke and the third of our sheep died and thursday the .29. a greate storme and satterday the .31.

the first of februarie whit calved gentile calved the ,11. of februarie it was wensday.

The twelvth month is februarie and hath .28. days being the yeare 1656 and the first yeare after the leape yeare sabath day the first monday the .2. called Candelmas day and sabath day the .8. and monday the greate snow fell tusday I came whom and sabath day was the .15. monday the .16. I fetched up the Reeke of hay and sabath day the .22. monday the .23. it was wet and satterday the .28. and the last day of this month Browne begin to mend.

The .19. of februarie Browne calved being Thursday.

The first month is march and hath .31. days being the year 1657. and the second yeare after the leape

yeare and sabath day the first berie calved the .24.
of februarie Colie calved the .6. day we changed .2.
bushels of winter wheate with my ffather for .2·
bushels of sumer wheate to sow and sabath day the
.8. and sabath day the .15. the Sacrament was administred Mr Thomson and his wife came and we lay at
Jams Averies and sabath day the .22. the meeting
was at my ffathers and the night before pidie calved
the .28. day the mare folled and sabath day the .29.
tusday the .31.

The second month is Aprill and hath 30 days wensday the first thursday the .2. i made an end of sowing of wheate upon the plaine the same day the two
heighfors did Calvie and wensday the .8. I had done
plowing for Indean Corne and that day I sowed flax
and feched up the hay friday the .10. I first kept the
Cattell abroad and yt same day I made an end of
planting Indean corne tusday the .14. we had the .2.
shots from goodman shaws wensday the .15. Thomas
time begun with James Averie thursday the .16.
Browne died monday the .20. we made the Contrie
Rate wensday the .22. and wensday the .29. we made
an end of cutting Clobboardes and thursday the .30.

The third month is may and hath .31. days and
friday the first and friday the .8. I had made an end
of cleaving of bolts the .13. day was the first lecttuer

at shaws friday the .15. I was apointed to go to the courte and friday the .22. I was at hartford and friday the .29. I came whome and delivered a firkin of butter to Thomas huet to carrie to simon Cobden sabath day the .31.

The .2. of June we first Trained at misticke 1657 The .8. of June I paid Mr Blinman .54.£ of buter yt 7 s.

The fourth month is Jun-e and hath .30. days monday the first wensday the .3. mr Blinman was to com to our house the day before I hedged for mr Tomson thursday the .4. I was at naraganset and monday ye 8 I was at Towne major mason was there and Captaine denison friday the .12. John went to Coneticut and monday the .15. and monday the .22. mr newman the day before taught at pequit and monday the 29 tusday ye .30. I was at seabrooke mill.

The fift month is July and hath .31. days wensday the first the second day being thursday I came from sabrooke mill wensday the .8. the day before I begun to mow the same day the meeting was at Towne about misticke and poquatucke ye lecter was this .8. day of July & wensday the .15. we puled hemp and I mowed ye major & Mr Brewster met at nayanticke and I was pressed and wensday the .22. I was reaping of winter wheate and the first lectter was prched at pequit & wensday the .29. I had fetched in all the winter wheate ther was .26. scoors of sheaves & friday the .31. & sowed .2. days turneps the 28 day of this month.

The sixt month is Agust and hath .31. days satterday the first & satterday the .8. I begun to reape at ye plaine and had sowne all ye turneps & plucked the flax & mowed meadow at ye head of ye creecke & satterday the .15. we made the wheate mowe I was ill in my throate yt weecke Ephraim had the ague & satterday ye .22. I opened ye well and Samuel grover fetched ye goate away & the lamb & satterday .29. Epharaim went to poquotucke Monday .31.

The 20th of Januarie being wensday mr Blinman gave nottis yt he would be gone.

The seventh month is september and hath .30. days tusday the first and monday the .7. I made an end of mowing of .31. loads of hay & tusday the .8. and tusday the .15. the goats were lost & tusday the .22. I begun to gather coren & tusday the .29 and mickelmas day & wensday the .30.

paid to goodman loungden nine shillings & two pence in Tallow Cheese & one shilling of wampum to carie.

The eight month is october and hath .31. days thursday the first and thursday the .8. I was at Nayanticke with Johns things & could not get them carried and Ephraim and Joseph begune to gather stalks I brought whome the toungs & thursday the .15. I had sown the winter wheat & friday and satterday I had been in the woods looking calves thursday the .22. & sabath ye .25. ye ministers seate was pulled downe ye .26. I killed ye swine ye ram was let loos thursday .29. we had .45. bushells of turneps cut satterday .31.

The ninth month is november and hath .30. days sabath day the first and sabath day the .8. and sabath day the .15. I was at pvidence with the merchants and wensday the .18. day I came from Towne thursday the .19. I thresbed Indean corne for to go to mill and sabath day the .22. monday .23. I was looking the canoow wensday the .25. I fetched the Cloth from harrises sabath day the .29. monday the .30. end.

The tenth month is december and hath .31. days and tusday the first and satterday the .5. I brought whome the Calves and tusday the .8. I was at poquanump & tusday the .15. I was cleaving of clapbords and tusday .22. I made an end cleaving of clapboards & begun to hew wensday I gave my wife phisicke & friday the .25. and Christmas day & tusday .29. and thursday the .31. I made an end of doing the side of my house with clapbords.

the .30. day was wensday and a day of thanksgiving at shaws.

The Leventh month is Januarie and hath .31. days and friday the First and friday the .8. the meeting was at misticke and I made an end of threshing the sumer wheat that was at first in the baren it was a snow the .2. snow & tusday the .12. hanah burned her hand & friday the .15. I had got ribs for the house and friday the .22. I wrought wt Aron Stark I agreed with herman garek about my canoow the .29. mr Blinman went this weeke to new haven there was .2. meetings at pequit mr Brewster p'mised me land for my mony sabath day the .31.

The twelvth month is februarie and hath .28. days and is the second yeare after the leape yeare and the yeare 1657 Thomas Minor and monday the first and monday the .8. I was at Towne for maries Cloths I sent a letter to John Joseph had the measles I had begun the hay reeke out by the creecke the .12. being friday white Calved .2. kids died and monday the .15. I was ill on my backe & monday the .22. wensday .24. I continued ill wensday .25. the misticke peopell went to towne to the meeting & wee had aleven kids & lambs sabath day the .28. we had .22. Kids and

.9. lambs and .3. Calvs Clement and Thomas was heare at the meeting.

The first month is March and the third yeare after the leape yeare and hath .31. days Monday the first I threshed winter wheate and monday ye .8. day this weecke wee threshed the indean (corn) we had .20. bushells and wheate .16. bushels and monday the .15. I set forth for stratford and monday the .22. and monday the .29. I was at nayanticke with my plow Irons and wensday the .31. it was a publike fast the Colt was lost.

because that the bay men begun in an unjust way to lay out mens lands that they had in possession before the things wer wholy ended maks me to turne wholy to Coneticut & and give them my list. The yeare 1658.

The second month is Aprile and hath .30. days Thursday the first the sixt day the mare folled and thursday the .8. I brought whome the hay from Burows we suncke the Canoows and Thursday the .15. the day before there was a snow friday the .16. Clement came whome satterday we mended the fence and thursday the .22. I had plowed one acker of ground in the plaine mr willis was heare mistris Blinman was loading to goo away. I p'mised mr willis to mow at poquatucke and if he give me as full power

as mr hains did and to keep 12 or 15 cattell there wt
his 12 or 15 and be at halfe cost in looking to them
the next winter & thursday .29. we made an end of
planting & brought whome the Colt.

The thirde moneth is may and hath .31. days saterday the first and satterday the .8. we had done
hewing of shingell we washed the sheep we had
mended the baren friday ye .14. we had shoren the
sheep we was at Tagwouncke we had plowed .2.
ackers in the plaine & satterday the .15. there is a
Church meeting at Towne & satterday the same day
o'r father was taken sicke & satterday the .22. we
had done plowing quite cros the plaine o'r father begun to mend friday .28. set cabbish plants we had
weeded o'r flax & sumer wheate & satterday the .29.
we wer to make a yard at tagwoncke monday .31.

The foureth moneth June .30. days tusday the
first satterday the .5. I sowed hay seed the Captain
came from Bostown Courte of Eleltion tusday the .8.
I was digen of a seller and that weeke we walled it &
tusday the .15. we made an end of the stone wall
thursday the .17. Captaine denison mr stanton goodman cheesbrough was heare to bid me to com to a
meeting and monday the 21 I was Called to veiw the
dead body of William Bostuck being by the Jury
conceived to be poysoned and tusday the .22. Jams

morgan was to go into the bay for A minnester and tusday the .29. I had carried Raymonds butter wensday the .30 we covered the seller and had hilled our coren and sowed turneps in the plain.

The fifte moneth is July and hath .31. days Thursday the first we wer going to Tagwoncke to mow because yt Roger was not redie and tusday the .6. day I went with Roger to poquatucke and there was a greate parte of the meadow cut and set up in small cocks and so I came whome againe and medled not and thursday the .8. I axled the cart and thursday the .15. I had cut the pease we had fetched the hay from the Creeke it rained the .14. day and thursday the .22. I had been at towne and agreed with mr brewin and made all even with him and killed the Ram we were Reaping of winter wheate and thurscay the .29. satterday the .31. we came from fishers Iland we weighed the woll for the workmen.

The sixth moneth is Agust and hath .31. days sabath day the first and monday the second I paid the butter to Raymond for the peuter saterday the .7. I sowed turnips and sabath day the .8. I had no optunitie to get my hay since we were at fishers Iland sabath day the .15. and satterday the .21. the wolf killed a lamb and sabath day the .22. I herd that

Bartlet was dead & sabath day the .29. tusday .31.
I was going to Bostown.

the last week in Januarie or thereabout there wer
five bound to their good behavior John Russell a
prisoner and bound.

The seaventh month is September and hath .30.
days wensday the first & wednesday the .8. and wednesday the .15. and wednesday the .22. I was com
whome from the commissionors on thursday the .23.
& wednesday the .29. and mickelmas day thursday
the .30. wee made an end gathering of Indean Corne.

The .21. of october being thursday John Minor was
married at Stratford.

The eight moneth is october and hath .31. days
friday the first friday the .8. John & Clement went
to Stratford sabath day the .11. of this month I
was taken sicke at goodman loungdens and monday
the .12th I tooke my bed friday the .15. I continued
sicke & friday .22. I was sicke. & friday .29 sabath
day .31. I continued sicke and the 10th of this month
I left Amos a firkin of butter at c'oem bins.

The ninth moneth is november and hath .30. days
monday the first and monday the .8. I was sicke
monday the .15. I was sicke & monday the .22. the
first day that I begun to sit up the 23 was tusday
Captaine denison & his man was heare I submitted

my selve to the Towne of misticke & poquatucke
being called southern Towne by the Court yt day
being read to me and monday the .29. tusday the
.30. I had not been abroad then the first snow fell &
monday

The tenth moneth is desember and hath .31. days
wensday the first day and the second day yt we had
cleaved pals sabath day the .5. I first went abroade
but everie night continued burning and weake wensday the .8. Thomas huet was at misticke we had a
goat died friday the .10. I was at my fathers & wensday the .15. I was abel to bracke hemp a littell &
wensday ye .22. ye lord preserved us from fier I was
not abell to doe any thing abroad and satterday the
.25. Christmas day the Captaine was arested & wensday the .29. we caried stufe for the cow yard friday
the .31.

The Leventh moneth is Januarie and hath .31.
days satterday the first and satterday the .8. I was
at towne sabath day the .9. the wolf killed .3. sheep
in the yard Tuesday the .11. we had whome all the
Cattel & hay and Satterday the 15. it was a thaw
and satterday the 22. Clement came from mill monday the .24. we made an end of corning hempe Satterday .29. monday .31. this weeke Clements heigher
Calved.

The .7. of Februarie I pruned trees good wife
grover was imprisoned John harwood Run away
Roger willisson was gone.

The Twelvth moneth is februarie and hath .28.
days and is the thirde yeare after the leape yeare and
the yeare 1658. and tusday the first and tusday the
.8. and tusday the .15. we had .4. lambs I begun to
Chop wt the folke & monday the .21 I was questioned
at my ffathers for being a leader to make division
2ly to take ye Captains power from him 3ly that (I
would) deliver the Captaine if he was demanded 4ly
for lightnes at Towne. We had 2 calved whit and
gentill tusday .22. Clement went to Towne & monday
the .28. & the last day and verie snowie Clement begun his time about the looms.

The first month is march and hath .31. days tusday the first and leape yeare and is the yeare .1659.
and tusday the .8. wee had made an end of cuting
pols we had six or 7 lambs tidy had caulved and
tusday the .15. we had laid all our logs in place
babomeden went to mill wensday the .16. my wife
was very sicke berie calved we had laid all the bottom logs to the Crecke and tusday the .22. I was at
sebrooke for slays and friday the .25. I came whome
being caled our ladie day we had .33. kids ye whit
heighfer had Calved & tusday .29. we had .40. kids

& we came from mr nickols wensday the 30 the general fast thursday .31.

The second month is Aprile and hath .30. days friday the first and friday the .8. we made an end of the orchard fence and grafting all yt I brought from seabrooke and spreading of mucke and friday the .15. I had sowed the peas and the .16. we sowed the wheate monday I came from the Towne Thomas fetched his loome thursday .21. Mr. Ades bought the .4. steers we wer pitching of stakes for the goat yard .6. kids lay out all night and friday the .22. tusday .26. sister hanah was maried ye .27. we made an end of the goats yard I was going to seabrook friday .29. satterday 30 I was at Sebrook for harnes and mr winthroup his family was there & mr willis.

The third month is may and hath .31. days sabath day the first I heard mr fitch & mr Blindman teach at seabrook the .29. of aprile wee lost .5. sheep and .12. kids that night by the wolfe it was wet and darke the .2. of may being monday Hanah had a son [in cipher] and sabath day the .8. goodman Burrows had sent the oxen he wrought them .8. days he said we had planted all the short lands in the plaine Amos and I made all even at John Bordens and sabath day the .15. we had made an end of planting John and his wife was heare and sabath day .22. satterday .28.

we made an end of the well and sabath the .29. and
tusday .31. we begun to weed the Corne simon Cobden was beare Mr winthroup & Mathew Griswold
ended the arbitration.

The foureth month is June and hath .30. days
wensday the first and wensday the .8. we covered the
seller sabath day the .12. Mr Tomson taught at mr
Burrows mr winthroup was there the .14. day we met
at bordens but did nothing wensday the .15. and
wensday .22. I received pay of mr Ades and thursday .23. my sons delivered the goats to mr perke for
his Coult and tusday .24. midsumer day misticke and
poquatucke men all agreed to act as one Towne and
wensday .29. I was at new london at a fast and
thursday the .30.

The fifte month is July and hath .31. days friday
the first and friday the .8. mr Blinman was at Towne
I made an end of hilling I carried the white Calve to
Burrows and friday the .15. we had begun one hay
reecke and satterday the .16. we finished the first
reecke of .6. Load the .10. of July Mr Blinman
taught at london and friday .22. tusday .26. I ow to
ye Towne 1-3-1. and friday the .29. we made an end
of Carrying of peas and sowed Turneps and sabath
day the .31. (we had 400 sheafes of wheat in the

Reeke and .320. sheafes in the baren & .3. loads of peas in the Reecke.)

The sixth month is Agust and hath .31. days monday the first the .2. day we got a load of wheate into house my wife tooke phisicke the fourth day we had all the wheate whome monday the .8th. Clement was heare and monday the .15. the .18. day we made the square Reecke and monday the .22. I plucked the winter hemp. The last of this month I was going to Connecticut the Commisinarie Court being there wensday the .31.

The seventh month is september and hath .30. days Thursday the first and thursday the .8. the .9th. day Johns son boren and thursday the .15. I was at Coneticut the .17. day I came whome and thursday .22. the mare came whome the gelden threw me friday mr willis & decon perke was at misticke (wita smith fetched the last of Captaine denisons goats saterday) we begun to set up the pals of ye yard and thursday the .29. caled mickelmus day the grt storme the 2 day before there was a meeting to send to mr peerson to chuse new commissinors friday the 30.

The eight month october and hath .31. days satterday the first and satterday the .8. we had 4 loads of Coren John and his wife came the .4th. of this month the .11th. day I made an end of husking the first .4.

loads and saterday the .15. tusday the .18. we had all our Corne whome the .24. we had the Cow of goodman nichols .25. we made an end of harvest we had .350 Trusses the .26. we had received .17. bushells of corne and .7. bushells of beans from the Indeans satterday 29. monday .31.

The ninth month is november and hath .30. days tusday the first I dlivered berie to goodman Nickols and brought whome John Kows and tusday the .8. we were at Mohegon the .14. day we had a court we wer carrying of doung tusday the .15. the .16. day Marie went to goodman nicols and tusday .22. My wife had that fit of sicknes with the Redspots .23. we kiled the beare 24 there was a towne meeting at smiths and tusday .29. we begun the brigd at the creeck at rivers head and ended the .30. being wensday

The tenth month is december and hath .31. days Thursday the first and thursday the .8. we had a day of thanksgiving and tusday we were to meet at Cheesbroughs house the five men. & thursday the .15. we wer geting of boults friday .16. I went to Captaine Denison to gree wt Thomas Perk about the meetting house and thursday 22 I was threshing of indean corn sabath day 25 and Christmas day there fell a great snow and thursday 29 satterday 31.

The leventh month is Januarie and hath .31. days

sabath day the first that weeke I threshed Indean corne and tusday and wensday the 3 & 4 day we met at my ffathers and I first heard of the third writting and disclaimed it and sabath day the .8. it snowed mr Smith had left the sabath and sabath day the .15. monday the .16. I begun to thresh whit pease and sabath day .22. we had no meeting & sabath day the 29 Captaine Denison did exercise monday the 30 the Commissioners met at Cheesbroughs tusday the 31 it is agreed that the Commissioners shall meet at mr Smiths the last 2 day of march & so the same of may.

The twelvth month is februarie and is the leap yeare being the yeare .1659. and hath .29. days wensday the first & wensday the .8. wee met at mr stantons the .6. & wensday the 15 we made an end of sawing the first stocke of boards tusday 21 we had a towne meeting about the meeting house & wensday 22 we were to begin the line at weekapoug & wensday the 29. we wer runing the towne line the 2 of march we came whome.

The first month is march 31 days & is the first yeare after the leape yeare being the yeare .1660. & Thursday the first & thursday the .8. John russell rune away the same time our frame was raised wensday the .14. we ended the courte thursday the .15. I was threshing of wheate for Ralpth perker we had

our .3. pigs from ffathers & thursday the 22 I paid
the last wheat our goats begun to kid Thomas huet
vessell was tached & tusday the .27. John Carried
all aboard thursday the .29. saterday .31. we had
built our backe & oven.

The second month is Aprile 30 days & sabath day
the first and sabath day the .8. we had begun the last
weeke monday the .9. Clement went to new london
to worke sabath day the .15 monday the .16 we made
an end of sowing the wheate & pease & tusday the
.17 we wer to set forth for the day & sabath day the
.22. the .20th. of Aprill we received a letter of Johns
safe arivall monday .23. we begun to plant & wensday .25. I made an end of all our plowing &
sabath day .29. monday the .30. we had made an end
of planting of our Indean Corne.

The third month is may 31 days & tusday the first
the .7th. day I was at the Towne the london ship was
at New london tusday the .8. I made the hedg at
the stand & wensday the .9. I made an end of yt
worke the .10th. & .11th. I shingled the north side
of the house & tusday the .15. & tusday ye .22. we
had kept a day of humiliation the day before the 24.
being thursday we were to set forth for the bay we
came to Bostowne the 30th & thursday the 31 ms
dier was Executed.   4568

The fourth month is June 30 days & friday the first I was at Bostowne friday the 8th I was at Bostowne & friday was .15. I lay at the trading house I set my hand to ye agreement between Major Alerton & the other englisg & the .3. narraganset sachems about the land Isacke willy was married that day sometime before & yt day pmised Amos Richerson .3 Cattell one blacke Cow one bull wt a white face .3. years ould one red steere of 2. years ould the 21. daay by the Courte a day of humiliation friday the .22. & friday .29. I paid pepeions ten shillings for killing of two woulfes & satterday the .30.

The fift month is July 31 days & sabath day the first this weeke I agreed with Rogers about Johns 2 Cows & a calfe & sabath day the .8. the 7th of this month I sowed turneps the 13. there (was) a towne meeting & sabath day the .15. I puled hemp Ephraim & Joseph mowed in the orchard friday & saterday .20. & 21. wee had a courte at Captaine denisons sabath day .22. 23. I looked horses fetched one loade of hay & satterday the .28. I cut pease & sabath day 29. & tusday the .31.

The sixt month is Agust 31 days & wensday the first I cut fense & caried them wensday the .8. I caried my wheate thursday the .9. I carried the Ram to the Iland & wensday the .15. friday .17 Thomas

& Ephraim was at Samuell Cheesbroughs the .13. day I had the geldin at Captaine denisons the 20th day John Tower came heare & wensday the .22. we Caried 5 loads of hay & made a reecke next to the baren wensday 29 I was at towne & tooke up things for John I was at preutis to shew the hors friday .31.

The seventh month is september 30 days & satterday the first mr winthroup was at new london the 4th day the horses wer at Culvers John moore begune to worke for me satterday the .8. the .12. I reckned wt mr picket and made all even being wensday & satterday the .15. Clement & John more went to new london I & Joseph was at bordens & the .2. horses were gone ye 12th day also I paid toung his silver befor Josias willkins and quite freed the horse & saterday the .22. I clove Clabords sabath day .23. we first did see Carries Cow to spring uder John was heare The last of september we came whome from narraganset & master brigden first taught heare.

The eight month is october 31 days & monday the first this day hanah her child died before day & monday the .8. the moone was Eclipsed I was to goe with mr Brigden toward mohegon & monday the .29. I caried the firkin of butter to Mr Smith for Amos I marked the Colt a bay mare without any white the mare have a white face a slit in the righte yeare .3

white feet parte of the .42. a whit ring about eatch yeare a halpenie on each yeare wensday the 31.

The ninth is november 30 days & Thursday the first friday the .2. I weighed Amos his firkin of butter at mr Smiths it was .70. pound & there is .13 pound to pay the .8. day being thursday we had Caried .45. loads of mucke out of the yards there was a meeting to be at smiths of the whole Towne. & thursday the .15. this weeke we killed the steere I was at new london & had the axes & guns mended the steere came to six pounds the .20. we begun the litel house thursday .22. it snowed the second time thursday the .29. we apointed a meeting to be at Cheesbroughs that day fourtnite I begun to cleane clopbords friday the 30 we had whome all the timber for the litel house.

The tenth month is december 31 days & satterday is the first & satterday the .8. I came from Coneticut the .13. day the Townes men met at Cheesbroughse & satterday the .15. the 11th of this month we raised the littel house tusday the .18. there is a courte at Captain denisons & saterday the .22 we got stones for the Chimbley monday 24 the Towne men met at Mr. Stantons tusday ye 25. caled Christmas day & satterday the .29. monday the .31. sabath day the

30 I received a letter from Cambrigde Christmas day
I received a letter from my Cousin in England.

The leventh month is Januarie 31 days & tusday
the first thursday the .3. we killed the sow tusday the
.8. I made an end of Threshing of the wheate in the
north end of the barne the same day it snowed I had
.20. Bushels of wheate Marie was sicke & tusday the
.15. Marie continued verie sicke & I fetched honie at
starts & tusday the .22. thursday .24. marie died
aboute six oclocke we had 40. bushells of wheate we
fetched in the pease & tusday the .29. I Reckned
with my ffather palmer there was all paid and .17.
shillings due to me thursday the .31. we had .10.
bushells of white pease.

The twelvth month is februarie and hath 28 days
friday the first aud is the first yeare after the leap
yeare & is the yeare .1660. this weeke Clement &
Thomas went to Stratford the white heighfer Calved
we finished the fence to the Rocks by the swampe
friday the .8. there fell a greate snow & friday the
.15. I made an end of Comming of hemp & friday the
.22. it hayled.

The second of march I sent to Aron Start to com the
.11. of march and renew the bounds between us and
he sent me word he would not till the major did com

The first month is march .31. days friday the first
and is the second yeare after the leape yeare & the
yeare 1661. This weeke we got poles for the fence
and friday the .8. Clement fetched whome his red
calfe and wee laid all the bottom poles by the well
Tusday the .12. I sowed two pecks of peas friday the
.15. I begun to make hedge at the Creecke & our
Indean begun his time & friday the .22. perke calved
I made hedg at the garden the day before I paid mr
loveland .15. pecks of wheat & 10 pecks to the smith
& one to Carie & friday the .29. I made an end of
the hedge in the pastor sabath day 31. we begun the
last Reecke of hay.

The second month is Aprile .30. days the first is
monday thursday the .4. we had sowed our peas &
wheate one bushell & halfe the Towne all met at
smiths Collie calved & monday the .8. wee had done
sowing wheate I planted apel trees Tusday the 9 the
select men met at shas we spent .8s wensday the
.10th. we met at Cheesbroughs to send to mr Brigden
monday the 15. I made an end of plowing for Indean
Corne. it was verie Could and verie littell grass monday .22. we begun to plant in the plaine & tusday 23.
we made an end and saterday .27. Capta(in) gookin
his Cattell came to me monday 29. I kept the Cattell
& tusday the 30. I kept Cattell Thomas perke said
mr Stanton had quanaquantago.

The third month is may .31. days & wensday is the
first this weeke the Captaine and I wer at new london
they denied us the records till they did heare from
the govenor and Courte the 7th day we brought the
line to misticke and wensday the .8. and friday the
.10th we run it to Cheesbroughs river the first line
gives all the meadow and all: the second all the upland wt out ye meadow monday the .13. the meeting
house was raised wensday the .15. I was at my father
palmers the .17. day being friday I am to set forth
for the bay.

at a court at Shaws John Borden was fined .25£.
John benit & his wife whiped upon the .13th of June
1661.

The fourth month is June 30 days & the first is
satterday wensday the 12. I came from the bay there
was a court at shas and when we came to see James
bemis his testimonie and peeter blacthfelds was
brought in I came away The .13. of June we had two
Calved killed in the pastor the .12. I came from bostowne and mr brigden saterday the .15 the .19 day
mr Richersons house was Raised satterday the 22.
saterday the 29. Captaine gookin was heare this
weeck we laid out walter palmer his land yt was given
to Captain denson and sabath day the 30.

The fift month is July .31. days monday the first

the 2 day we had a courte at Cheesbroughs wensday I was (at) sebrooke wt mr winthroup and friday I went to mr Stantons and prised the Catell monday the .8. I fetched the green ginger wensday the .10. it was a day of publike thanksgiving and monday the .15. I cut the pease our folke was making hay at tagwouncke the .17 day I was to go to fishers Iland to prise Catel and monday the .22. I plowed for turneps at the plaine & monday .29. we made an end of reaping wheate the 30th we had all in it rained about noon: we had .900. sheaves of wheate wensday the .31

The sixt month is Agust .31. days & thursday the first and thursday the .8. our Indean went from us our sons wer at the Captains at reaping. Captaine gookin his calfe was bit 2 days before and the 14 day we Cacth the wild horse & Court was at Coneticut thursday the 15 & thursday the 22. we had a Courte at shas the damage came to 6 saptie & thursday the 29. goodwife galop was heare saterday the .31.

friday the .16 of Januarie 1662 The Couldest day that yeare: The 21 day noosacke The Indean was sent to the bay & had fiftie shillings.

The seventh month is september .30. days & sabath day the first the commissionors was heare major masson spake in the meeting house sabath the 8th we had made an end of hay making monday I gathered hops & the 14 day I Commed flax my sons was all about the Cart & wheels sabath day the 15th good-man Cheesbrough spake to me about moving mr Brigden from fathers deaken parke was heare & sabath day the .22. monday 23. we Caught the wild horse the 20th of this month mr picket & we parted the sheep

The eight month is october .31. days tusday the first friday the 4th my wife & I came from the bay the 7th day being monday I received .3. mares by george Robinson tusday the .8th the .10th I solde the wilde horse monday the .14th. I and John was at Towne made all even between tounge and John and John owed tonge eight shillings & tusday the 15. & tusday the 22. wensday a day of thanksgiving at new london the .26. day John Galop tooke the testimonie of Jogn benet tusday 29. thursday 31.

The ninth month is november .30. days friday the first the fifth tusday Clement said his mare was prest for to goe to Bostowne & saterday the 23 I came whome and thursday the .28. there was a Towne meeting & new Choyce of Townesmen & othe(r) of-ficers at mr smiths was this meeting

sabath day the 10th of november 1661 Walter palmer departed this world.

The 6th of December it was agreed by the Commissinors at Cheesbroughs that the 12th day at shas
the oath of fidelitie should be tendered to all that
would tak it & mr stanton consented.

The tenth month is desember .31. days sabath day
the first thursday the fiffe we had a Towne meeting at
Cheesbroughs sabath day the .8. the 10th day we
agreed at shas to build a mill at Cheesbroughs the
12th day being Thursday John & his wife and childe
was to goe away sabath day 15. the 18 & 19. day we
made bridges the .17 day we killed our swine The
sabath day .22. the 23. we were at mothers to see mr
Brigden sabath day 29. the 30 we had our Catell to
tagwouncke tusday the 31.

The eleventh month is Januarie .31. days wensday
the first the 2 day I was at poquatucke the 3 day I
clove shingell & wensday the .8. the .9. day I & my
wife was to see mr Brigden the 10 day it snowed
wensday tho 15. the snow was all of the ground the
.13. day being monday we fetched sam & hanah ther
heighfer from Arons & wensday the 22. mr Brigden
was at poquatucke Thomas & Joseph was at new
london The .26. day I was at new norwitch I came
whome lame wensday 29. Ephraim & Joseph went
(to) tagwouncke friday the 31. we had out Catell all
whome.

The twelvth month is februarie .28. days satterday
the first and the yeare .1661. and the second yeare
after the leape yeare thursday .6 day I reckned with
John mors and satterday I was at poquatucke at mr
Stantons my wife mother & Brother Elihu being the
.8. day & saterday the 15. Josepth swimed for the
Canoow and Clement was looking the mares I was
threshing of wheate & saterday the .22. we treshed
the gray pease. 5 peckes I was verie lame in my back
the 20th day John mores was taken by the Constabel
there was a Courte the 25 and 26. at shas being tuesday and wensday : friday 20. I was verie ill our sister
hanah was very weake Clement was at the westward.

The first monteh march & hath 31 days saterday
the first & is the third : yeare after the leape yeare
and the yeare 1662. monday the .3 day I and Joseph
was looking mares at poquatucke 4 days tusday
Thomas was at new London friday the 7th goodman
starts Indean came to him saterday the .8 tusday the
11th we made an end of framing at starts our whit
calvfe died saterday the 15 I was ill in my head the
16. day I tooke phisicke the 19 day was a towne
meeting about mr Brigdon and satterday the 22. the
23 I began to mend & satterday .29. monday the
.31. Thomas was looking the mares at Naraganset &
his Coult was brought whome.

The second monteh is Aprill & hath 30. tusday the
first wensday the .2. Samuell & hanah heighfer went
to the majors Iland Tusday the 8th Thomas first fell
sicke at narraganset as he was looking the mares The
.12 day satterday I begun to sow pease & Tusday
the 15. I sowed peas thursday I went to narraganset
being the 17 day satterday the 19. Thomas departed
(this life.) sabath being .20 he buried The 22. tusday I came whome & brought the mare & Coult &
Tusday the .29. I sowed oates my wheat was sowed
& wensday the 30. The .24th. of this month mr
Brigden departed this life.

The third moneth is may & hath 31 days thursday
the first I planted Indean Corne The Charge of the
yeare past 1661 this day cast up coms to 101-00-00
besides the diet of the family The .6. day we lost a
Coult The .7. day we made an end of plowing Thursday the .8. & thursday the .15 I was at Stratford
thursday the .22. I came whome friday the .23. we
planted againe what was pulled up : & thursday 29. I
was at new london and brought the Chest & boxes &
glass & nails saterday 31 I was at goodman cheesbroughs.

The 24th of June 1662. I was at warweek for the
mare shee cost me 3-8-0

The fourth moneth is Jun & hath 30 days sabath

day the first we had all our kids killed monday ye second I received 2 letters from my Cousin William sabath day the .8. I was at norrig (Norwich). Ephraim was sicke the 13 day I saw hartleys house Raised & sabath day the 15 I was at new london mr Tinker wensday the 18th we had made an end of hilling friday the 20th I took up the childrens legacies I never saw the will of my ffather palmer till then sabath day 22. the 25 I came whome with the mare sabath day the 29th monday the 30 the 27 being friday we had acount for dartes indeans.

The fifth moneth is July & hath 31. days tusday the first & saterday the 5 we had made a .11. loads of hay at Tagwouncke we then saw & heard of all the mares but the litel blacke mare Tusday the .8. I went to Caring of hay at the farms friday the 11th. we fenced the .3. Reecks & it rained & Tusday ye 15 I cut peas & yt day the Calfe was taken ill as the Indean was keeping it wensday night he died & Tusday the 22 we were at shas to meet with holsie The 23 we sowed turneps The 29. was tusday we begun to reape I went to goodman Cheesbrough about mr Chance thursday 31.

The sixt moneth is August & hath 31. days friday the first & friday the 8 we got our fouerth Reeke of hay togeather at Tagwounke & friday the 15. mr

Chancy came to Towne: The wensday before Rogers
spake to the Church The 20th day being wensday I
& my wife both dreamed: we made an end of hay
makeing friday 22 I was taken ill in my shoulders as
I was gathering 2 trees of apples The 25th Sarah was
at Smiths Tusday 26. I was at Narraganset for witnes
about the mares friday 29 mr Chancy was heare
sabath day the last mo

The seventh moneth is september & hath 30. days
Monday the first I was to set forth to the Commish-
onors Courte at Bostowne The 20th day I came
whome & the 22 I was at New London Clement &
ffrancis willie was made Monday 29 & michelmus day
it Rained we wer gathering of Corne & tusday the
30. we wer all (at) the Towne at Captan denisons at
a feast.

The eight moneth is october & hath 31 days wensday the first The 2 day we made an End of gathering
of Indean Corne and wensday the .8. we came from
shammatucke thursday the .9th we fetched 24 bushell
2-1 of Coren from soonamoten wensday the 15 I was at
new london and had the horse shew set tusday 21 we
got clab board mr stanton showed me the Rate from
Coneticut wensday 22 the Towne met about the dam
& wensday .29. a day of Thanksgiving at new london

friday 31. I was at my mothers & we found Clements mare.

The ninth moneth is november & hath 30. days saterday the first ye .6. day I came from Rehobothe 7 day we met and it was discovered yt ye warant from Coneticut was left upon file on the bay saterday the .8. it was wet & satterday 15 I was at new london about the Irons & saterday 22 I was prparing to goe to bostowne with Clement we killed our swine the same day wensday .26. Clemet was married & I was taken ill in my backe & saterday the 29 & sabath day the 30 my wife was at new london. The 19 day mr Stantons Two daghters was married.

The tenth moneth is december & hath 31. days Monday the first I was still ill in my backe the celler was on fier Elisha went to the smiths for mill Irons the second Joseph carried the mucke out of the Calves yard The 8 day we had new Choice of officers I was left free it was agreed that ever after the Eletion should be on the first Tusday in December and monday the 15. I made an end of the winter hemp Ephraim was at Averies and monday 22 we made an end of fething of 20 load of wood monday 29. we had a meeting to read the Coneticut writings John Colver had turnips wensday 31 The 30 we had a courte and I was tried

The eleventh moneth is Januarie & hath 31. days
thursday the first we drove up the Catel to the farme
The second day I went to Elderkins the 5 day I and
my wife came whome the 6 day we had a lambe
Thursday the 8. the 4th snow The 15 day thursday
Clement was heare we had .4. pigs of burrows ye 16
day Cold Thursday 22. There was .6. snows fallen
The .21. day moosucke was sent to The bay we had 8
lambs ye .26. day Clements Red Calfe came : Thursday 29. there fell the ninth snow satterday the 31.

The 14th of februarie being satterday moosack
came from the bay : & valentines day.

The twelfth moneth is february and hath .28. days
sabath day the first and is the yeare 1662. and the
third yeare after the leape yeare and from the Creation the yeare .5611. monday the .2. it snowed wensday ffourth it snowed & saterday 7th it was the
12 snow and sabath day the .8. the 10th day it
snowed & I was ill wensday the .11th Christopher
was mending the harnes and sabath day the .15 there
fell the 14th snow the 16th day Ephraim went to new
london with the axe and sabath day the 22 monday
23. the .15 snow fell william was heare & 25 the
greate storme was

This present writting witnesseth that I Nehemiah

Roice shewmaker of new london doo heareby ingage
to supplie with shews Thomas Minor and his familie
for this yeare next insuing the date heare of as
foloweth begining at the first of march next till.
.1663. the first of march! viz: shews of nins at four
shillings six pence levens at five shillings six pence
twelves at six shillings and 13teens at six and six
pence if plaine or wooden heels also I Thomas Minor
doe heare by ingage to pay for all my shews in pease
or Indean Coren 3s p bushell wheate at 4s p bushell
buter & good murchatabell Cheese at 6d p pound if
the cheese be all new milke if not at five pence p
pound as witnes our hands this 20th of februarie
1661.   Thomas Minor.
                  Neihemijan Royse.

The 23. of februarie being tusday 1663 the third
meeting of the Towne when they drew lots and
granted Twentie lots of an hundred ackers appece.
I an my sons had none and Tusday the first of march
.64. the .4 meeting John Gallop was Chosen Towns-
man and The Captain left out as I was tould.

The 26. of november 1662. being wensday Clement
& Ffrancis wer married.

The .19. of Januarie .1663. being Tusday Clements
Daughter Marie was Borne at nayantick.

The Last of november .1672. Clements Daughter Ann was borne.

The 6th day of December .1672. his wife ffrancis Departed this Life.

The .27. of october .1662. I had ffrom the Indeans three score and seventeen bushells of Corne that was our halfe of what they planted that yeare.

The 16. of februarie 1663. John Benit died and was Buried the 18 day.

The first of Januarie 1663 four Cattell was Driven to the farme the 24. of februarie being wensday The Cattell came whome.

The 29. of July 1667 Mr noyce and I Reckned and he was to have the Cow I had of Williams and I was to pay his passages this yeare at Carie lathams for his 3-18-1-2-1 and all things between us were even.

Thomas Minor.

The first month is march and hath 31. days sabath day the first and is the year 1663 and from the Creation the yeare .5612 and leape yeare wensday the .4th heare came 4 men John genings shewmaker and one Christine they said they came from long Island The 7. day being satterday I brought whome the Catell from the farme sabath day the .8. the 11th day Joseph paid weldman wheate & sabath day the 15th. I was at new london monday the .16. Captaine moris was heare Christopher begun to weave The .18 day we begun to hew timber at the farme sabath day (22 23) the marshell Read the instructions and Charter and sabath day 29. ye Cooper was at meeting Tusday .31. I was at mr Brusters monday the 6 of Aprile 1663 we tooke mr Amos his horse.

The second month is Aprile & hath 30. days wensday the first a day of humiliation at norwich friday I came whome and wensday the .8. we sowed pease thursday the .9. we grafted 100. trees Tusday we sowed the white pease wensday the .15. we sowed oats The 16 day being Thursday The Bay mare folled I and my wife was [at nayanticke friday it snowed sabath there was no meeting wensday 22. I was at the Iland stubing wensday 29 The 30 day we Raised the house at Tagwouncke.

The third month is may & hath .31. days friday the first I had my cloaths from Codner the 5 day tusday the mill went mr smith came by: Elderkin went whome friday the .8. I made an end of plowing the wheate stubell The Captain house was raised. Ephraim was at new london with ffrancis and friday the .15 I made an end of plowing the 16. we made an end of planting Clement was sicke friday the 22 we had

Clobborded the sides of house at the farme and friday 29. and Josepth was at seconcke Thomas Sloue his wife and Jonas palmer was heare sabath day the 31.

The fourth month is June & hath .30. days monday the first it was wet and monday the .8. I fetched bees from burrows our backe at the farme was made monday the 15. wee weeded the Coren The 16 day I was with Comstock for my pitch forks the 19 day I lent goodman stricklen one bushell of corne and goodman williams monday 22. the Captain was com whome I weeded the hops Joseph was to End mr Richersons house my wife was sicke saterday 28 I went to Coneticut monday 29. tusday 30 I was at mr willis & Deacon parke met me at mr stons house

The fifte month is July & hath .31. days wensday the first monday the 6th I came whome from Coneticut Captaine morrice was a prisnor at Arons wensday the .8. Samuell Cheesbrough brought The Execution and the 14 day I was with Thomas Bell wensday the 15 The 16. day was the Training The sabath day 19. mr fflecher taught and the 20 day we caried a way the 4. rams The 21 I recived a leter by soona] mooten from John our sister hanah was heare and wensday 22. The 23 I sowed the Turnops monday 27 The cart went to the farme to cary hay I begun to cut pease tusday 28 I carried butter to Weldman a cheese to culver and wensday 29. friday 31. at night the Thunder like a gun.

The sixth month is Agust & have .31. days satterday the first I made an end of cuting of pease Thursday the .6. we had in all the pease and sowed turnops satterday the .8. we had a greate deliverance from fier we sowed Turnops and satterday the 15. the 16. goodman Cheesbrough Desired The inhabitants to meet for the setling of the ministrie and other things: wee had .700 sheaves of wheate .13 score without the Barne Ephraim was at new london the 15. 16. & 17 days & satterday 22. I was looking the horse monday 24. I was looking the horse sha sent for the Bwe and satterday 29. monday 31. I went to mill and my wife was at gallops the .2. maids were naked.

The seventh monteh is september and hath .30. days Tusday the first it rained The second day I came from norwig Tusday the .8. mr ffletcher was heare monday the 14 we found our Calfes Tusday the 15. mother was heare the old (wo)man marie tincker the major had been at Cheesbroughs The 21. I made sider Tusday 22. and Tusday the 29 and mickelmas day There was a meeting about mr fflecher and to heare the news from the Commissinors wensday the 30.

The eight moneth is october & have .31. days Thursday the first Thursday the .8. I was at the generall Court Thursday the 15 I came whome The same day Aron starts Childe died & Thursday .22. Clement was heare The meeting was tusday when mupquatance was given to The ministry for ever 27 day being Tusday I found the Roane mare and shee had lost her Coalt & wednesday 28 was a day of thanksgiving Thursday 29 satterday thirtie one 31.

The ninth monteh is november & have .30. days sabath day the first monday the 2 we run the west bound of new london sabath day the 8. thursday the 12 we sould the mill sabath day the 15 Mr savage taught my Brother John was heare and sabath day the 22 it snowed we had no meeting 24 I diged parsneps The 28 we fetched pals sabath day 29. I came whome and we had no Exersies till Two or Three o'clocke Mr Stanton pformed Dutie Monday the 30

The tenth monteh is December & have .31. days Tusday the first there should have been a new Choice of all officers in the Towne Tusday The .8. Agedouset was at mr Tinkers and Tusday 15 I had my horse shewed at Badcoks the 19 day I ftcthed the Cowes back sabath day the 20. we had no meeting Tusday 22 we made an End of Cuting wood The Cow that was hanahs calved Ephraim had 2 bushells of wheate of mother Thursday the 25 and Christmas day Tusday 29 thursday 31. I was at naraganset.

The leventh monteh is Januarie & have .31. days friday the first & saterday the .2. I came whome from Naraganset friday the 8 we wer com from Clements the greate snow fell monday the 4 day Thomas stanton was taken prissnor & we had no meeting in three sabaths before friday the 15. I begun the thresh wheate & friday the 22 I was Threshing peas our Sister hanah was heare we tooke up the hogshead of Appels friday the 29. I made an end of Threshing whit peas we had 14 bushels & friday the 16 Clements Daughter was Borne

The Twelvth month is februarie & have Twentie and nine 29 days & is leape yeare monday the first day & is the years 1663 and from the Creation .5612 The second day Tusday the .2. mr stanton was heare to have me to help on the sabath day I was threshing gray peas it was candelmas day monday .8. tusday the towne meeting I had threshing of oates wensday the .10. goodman gallop laid out the bounds between the major and me and monday the 15. I made an end of threshing wheate tusday 16 masaseth was heare John Benit died and was buried the .18. day monday 22 and monday 29. we agreed for The wal to be made.

The first month is march & hath 31 days Tusday the first and is the yeare 1664 and the first yeare after

the leape yeare and from the Creation .5613. The day
of purgation and Tusday the .8. a day of humiliation
at new london and Tusday the .15. The .17 I made
an end of plowing at Tagwonk & Tusday .22. we and
moses rendered The bounds at Tagwonckee friday the
25. and Caled our lady day sabath day the 27 Captaine
morice marble and lamb lay heare Tusday 29 Thursday 31. 1664.

The 8th of Aprill 1664 I received mr Blindmans
letter

The second month is Aprill & hath 30 days friday
the first I begun to sow peas & to plow ould ground
& was at mill friday the 8. sabath day the 10. I was
at new london my wife was very sicke the 13 day a
fast publicke at Coneticut friday 15 The orchard was
planted the 16 the ground at the point was planted
friday .22. I garned satterday 23. we branded The .3
Coults The bay mare was wanting 27 manaseth &
francis Richard Datrs was heere friday the 29 we
made an End of sowing oats satterday the 30.

The third month is may & hath 31 days sabath day
first sabath day the 8. the 11 I wrot my leters for
England Clement & William nickhols was heare
Thursday the .12. I found the Roane mares blacke
Coult and marked it thus $\frac{T}{M}$ The 14 day I found the
Roane mare and a blacke horse Coult and marked it

and sabath day the 15 and sabath day 22. 23 & 24 There was Choice of millitarie officers at new london the 26 our horse was upon Cheepachewug The 27 day I found the ould mare and her Coult sabath 29 Tusday 31. morgan and John beebe was heare.

The fourth month is June & hath 30 days wensday the first I ground our last Corne and wheate & wensday The .8. I was to goe to Stratford mr plaisted (and) ould Cheesbrough was goeing to norig To surrender the Towne to Coneticut & wensday .15. I was at stratford The 18 day I had mr Richards leter being satterday my Brother william palmer was heare at worke aboute the Barne wensday the Tusday 28 we raysed the Baren mr noyce was heare wensday 29. Thursday 30.

The fift month July & hath 31 days friday the first and friday. the 8 I was at new london for shews and friday the 15. Richard dart was heare at worke I sent to the Iron works and to john by Secoggisbus squa my sone were mowing at the farme monday the 18. day I delivered gentill to philips in 5-5-0 & friday 22. I fecthed the 40 sheaves of oats in The 26 I sowed Turneps in the pease ground The 30 day being sater-day we ended our hay at The farme sabath day 31.

The sixt month is Agust & hath 31 days monday the first and monday the 8. we begun to reap wheat

Manaseh came hither the .9. day I saw houghs mare
and a stone Coult with her the .10. day Benit brought
the bay mare the .12. day friday we had cut our wheat
there was .1200. sheaves monday the 15 & Thursday
the 18. we had all our wheat and oats togeather we
had 460 sheeves of oats monday .22. 23. we had a
court car was summoned 29 monday I gathered apels
30 day tusday another court warned wensday 31.

The seventh month is September & hath 30 days
Thursday the first Clement was here Thursday I rode
with nathienall being the 8th day mr noise came and
his Brother the 12th day we wer at new london to pay
dart Thursday .15. I had gathered .120. bushells of
apels and pounded .6. barels of sider Thursday 22. we
had gathered all our Corne in the plaine we had our
Cows and Calves into the filde our Towne meets Thursday 29. and michelmas day friday the 30 The 24 day
Cap denison mried

The eight month is October & hath 31 days satterday the first and satterday the .8. John and his wife
and Clement and his wife was heare the 14 day John
and his wife and Children went away it was a storme
at night saterday the 15. friday the 28. I came from
Bostowne monday the 31. I sent Eight bushells of
Corne to Cary by pyatungus

The ninth month november & hath 30 days tusday

the first and Tusday the .8. I was at london paid John
keeny received a letter from John The .9. day we
planted tree and Tusday the .15. I went to mohegon
and Thursday 17. we brought the boardlogs Tusday
22. we begune to Clobboard the baren and Tusday 29
we came from norridge then we carried hanah then
fell the second snow wensday the 30th and a day of
thanksgiving.

The tenth month is December 31 days Thursday the
first & Thursday the .8. we saw the Blasing star mr
ward & Ensinge Averie was heare and Thursday 15.
and the 12th day being monday Joh(n) galop and
John Kar & Joh(n) Ascrut fought and Tusday the
20th Mr ward (&) mr Savage Returned to Bostowne
and Thursday 22. friday 23. mr dier went forth sabath
day 25. and Christmas day & Thursday the 29 an
Extreme could night satterday 31.

The leventh month is Januarie & hath 31 days
sabath day the first the 7 day we had our wheate and
pease and oats into the barnes sabath day the 8.
Thursday the 12th hanah came whome The 14 day we
sawed planck sabath the 15. the 16 a towne meeting
about the lists mr Cheesbrough said The Townes men
must take them: sabath day 22. & sabath day 29. mr
noice was sicke The 30. our Catell went to the farme
tusday the 31.

The Twelvth month is ffebruarie & hath 28 days wensday the first & is the first yeare after the leape yeare 1664. and from the Creation 5613. the 6 & 7 day I was at new london and paid picket peas 24 bushell & ½ wensday the 8. & it was wet wensday 15 I was at mill goodman dart went away the 21 mr noys & we had been wt mr ficth wensday 29 the great snow fell and Tusday the 28 1 was at mill.

The 14 day of Aprill 1665 we had sowed six bushells of white peas and Two bushells of gray pease in the orchard: the 17 day I sowed six bushels of oats in the plaine being monday.

The 20th: of Aprill 1665 our sister Rebecka was married mr savage grounded his sloope in the Cove The 25. of Aprill 1665 I made an End of sowing of wheat in the plaine five bushells & one pecke & one bushell of Barlley: 20 bushells one peck all.

The 21 of november 1666 I begun the yeare with Carie latham for fferring for this yeare ffollowing.

This 21 of november 1666 norwich men and Morgan was heare to lay out the Indean land at pachag or Elsewhere.

1665

The first moneth is march & hath 31 days wensday the first & is the second yeare after the leap year &

is The yeare of our lord 1665. and is from the creation 5614. I was warned to a towne meeting the 2 day to chuse officers I was at london for malasses and paid Richard dart I was informed by Edward ffanings of the broyle between Aron & Tho parke and John galop wensday The 8. heare should have been a courte and weusday 15. I was at naraganset with the Commiss-enors & wensday the 22. my horse was pressed sater-day 25. & our ladie day wensday the 29. a court was to be at poquatucke friday 31 the Commisinors went away

The second moneth is Aprile & hath 30 days sater-day the first I saw the Blassing star in the Est about the rissing of the day star: my horse was returned and satterday the .8. our neighbors came whome from warwicke monday the 10th I grafted the 11. 12 & 13 we sowed pease in the orchard & saterday 15. & satterday the 22. I had my horse shewed satterday the 29. our Brother william went away sabath day the 30.

The third moneth is may & hath 31 days monday the first I received a leter from John: it was our day for Choice of deputies for the Court Samuel Chees-brough and I was chosen monday the .8. we wer to set forth to Coneticut: monday 15 I was at Court Thursday I came whome from Coneticut being the 18 day monday 22 I set forth for Stratford & put back againe the 28 day I came whom from Stratford the 31 we washed the sheep being wensday.

The fouerth moneth is June & hath 30 days Thursday the first & this weeke George Tongue was sicke at shas & Thursday the .8. Captaine denison was heare takeing a view of writings & Thursday the 15 I was at mr Stantons house about takeing of Testimonies about Captaie Denison and John Car Munday 22. I was at the Courte Thursday 29. ffriday 30 I came from the Committe at london.

The fifte moneth is July & hat 31 days saterday the first I made and End of heaving the botoms of the hay reeks into the yard satterday the 8 I came from Coneticut Munday 10. I went to seaconcke & saterday 15 the 16 day I received my Cosin and mr Blindmans leters the 17 day Ephraim went to Seabrooke: the 15 day at night Tubs & Trebee lost car. I granted 2 warrants to the 2 Constables to search for Car saterday the 29 I had my whit pease in and sowed turneps in the orchard monday 31.

The sixth moneth is August & hath 31 days Tusday the first I sowed Turneps among the squashes the 3 days being Thursday I came from New london & my wife The 8 day Tusday & Thursday the 10 day we had our oats 400 shefes & 50. And fryday the 11 mr winthroup was heare The Three Townsmen mised To call a towne meeting and to setell the Indeans at Cowshuduke Tusday the 15 and friday the 18 The major was heare & goodwife sha p'msed to pay lam 30 s and tusday 22. the 25 and 26 The Commissonors met Tusday 29. I made the 2 barels of sider wensday .30 mr stanton was heare.

The 20th of november 1665 manaseth is to be with Thomas Bell for 6. moneth and to have 18 s p moneth and his diet: washen and lodging.

The first of Januarie 1665-66 (I) Branded the Coult of the ould mare a mare Coult collered between a browne and a blacke on the backe somewhat whitish under the bely all white from the Eies downward to the very mouth thus .3. The left and fouer white feet—a litel about the feter locks, and the Coult of my wives white faced mare, a stone Coult a browne bay with the left foot behinde white(e) with a litell blacke hair on both Sides of the foot between the hoofe and the white, both branded thuse in the left Buttocke ^T_M and a halpeny upon Each Eare

The last day of november 1665 The generall courtes order about horses being branded with a "K" was published and much opposed in our Towne by many: The 13 day of december being ffriday there was a day of humilliation kept at mr Richersons house.

The 28 day of november 1665 being Tusday I was at shas & he was not at whome & I asked 30 s of shas wife and Samuell Cheesbrough was there and forbid shas wife to pay it me and said that he would answer it at the Courte & Thomas Stanton Junior was A witnes Thursday The 28 day of December 1665. A Towne meeting the month being out that the Court order was published about branding horses I desired it might be atended Elisha Cheesbrough said it was but my Story there was no order for it, John Packer Edward faning was there.

The seventh moneth is september and hath 30 friday the first John Car Came to Samuel Cheesbroughs house. The Constable also there talked with him the 6 day I was at mr Stantons, I pressed the apell drinke friday the 8th heare was testimonies taken Sabath the 10 John Car was seen in our Towne and friday 15 I came whome with the sugar I am to pay mr noyce 5-11-8 the whole rate is 72-18-9. friday 22 friday 29. and mickelmus day saterday 30 The 28 day of this month we first Trained.

The eight moneth is october & hath 31 days sabath day the first and sabath day we p'fected the towne list sabath day the 15 I was at Coneticut sabath day 22. mr noyce Taught the first after his coming whome monday 23. goodwife lewis died and was buried

Tusduy 24. 28 day saterday I made an End of press-
ing sider sabath day 29 Tusday 31.

The ninth moneth is november & hath 30 days
wensday the first and wensday the 8th I was at the
Countie Courte aboute Car and ffithes wife and perks
and wensday the 15 I was come from the Countie
Courte and braking of hemp and thursday the 16 I
made an End of braking & wensday 22. 27 munday
we killed the Swine goodman lam and I reckned
Thursday the 30 day we trained the day before was
a day of thanksgiveing the 28 day I asked 30 s of sha
and Samuell Cheesbrough was there.

The tenth moneth is december and hath 31 days
friday the first I was at mill The weaver was heare
the 2 day Robert bartlet had atachment the 8 day is
friday The greate Tide that was 3 quarters of a yard
deep in our Celler Ephraim & Josepth was at the
farme the 14 day Thursday we had a private training
friday the 15 day I begune to thresh the 16 day I was
london friday 22 it was Exceeding Could my wife
was very sicke monday 25 and Christmas day our
Sister hanah was heare friday 29. saterday the 30
sabath day 31 thursday 28 we had a towne meeting
for rat(e)s

The eleventh moneth is Januarie & hath 31 days
munday the first we branded Two Coults hanah went

to mr denisons monday the 8th and thursday the 11
we had a towne meeting goodman sha received 37 s
of me as parte of my boat (2) the 13 day saterday
I made an end of winowing wheate I had 13 bushells
and monday the 15 we met with mr Noyes monday
22 it was verie Cold we had 30 bushells of oats the
25 being thursday I carried corn to mr Richerson
monday 29 we broched the barell of Sider my wife
feched malaces at mr Richersons wensday 31. the 30
day was verie wet

The twelfth moneth is ffebruarie and hath 28 days
Thursday the first and the second yeare after the
leap yeare 1665. & from the Creation 5614 The .6.
day mr Richardsons house was raised the 7. day a
great snow fell manaseth was heare agedousets
daughter was borne under a rocke the .8. day thursday & monday the 12 we had a towne meeting thursday 15—monday the 19 we had a towne meeting
Thursday 22 badcock lay heare 23. I was at poquatuck saterday 24 I made an end of Threshing peas
Tusday 27 we wer to heare the mr richersons maters.

The first moneth is march & hath 31 days Thursday the first 1666 & the third from the leape yeare:
and from the Creation .5615 2 day we had Towne
meeting for Electtion: our old mare died Thursday
8 day goodman Averie & morgan & their wives wer

heare the day before I was with mr noyce in ye woods and Thursday the 15. I was at lams my wheeles came from Tagwoncke monday 19 day hanah Averie was heare & Captaine denison John Gallop Aron start & the Constable I delivered the warrant for the rate £18. 3s. 0o at id yt wensday 21 the greate storme was Thursday 22.

Monday the 17 day of June 1667. I Received a Cow of williams Son, shee was blacke.

The second moneth is Aprill & hath 30 days the 1 day is sabath day The 7 day satterday I came from Norrige sabath day the 8. The 11th day wensday The macth was made up between Ephraim and hanah Averie I gave the 2 horses to Ephraim and Josepth to buy Their weding suts sabath day the 15 Sabath day 22 Ephraim and hanah Averic was put over the meeting house dore Saterday 28 I made an end of plowing sabath day 29 monday the 30 we had a towne meeting.

The third moneth is may & hath 31 days Tusday the first monday 7th I went to Coneticut Tusday the 8. Thursday the 10 day was the day of Electtion at hartford Tusday 15 I was at Coneticut Thursday 17 I came whome my wife was verie sick: and Tusday 22. Thursday 24 I and my wife was at Clements monday 28 we tooke up the bay mare & Eare marked the Roane mares Coult a blacke mare Coult with a star on the ffore head 29 day Tusday I received a leter from John by deliverance blackman my wife was at N. L. J G: H. G thursday the 31. we ar to Traine the 2 of June a towne meeting I was not warned to it.

The fourth moneth is June & hath 30 days friday the first wensday the 6 I went upon Sumons to the Countie Court saterday the .9. I came whome monday the 10. we killed the Calfe ffriday the 15. wensday the 20. our Ephraim was maried ffriday .22. friday 29 I fecthed siths from lams Saterday the 30 the majors mare & Coult was heare.

The fift moneth is July and hath 31 days Sabath day the first monday and Tusday the 2 & 3 days we rund the Townes bounds Thursday we had a towne meeting John Gallop and I Changed lots the 6 day we run the line from mistick to poquatuck the major was heare Sabath day the 8 & wensday the 11 John & manaseth went away sabath day the 15 ffriday the 20 we had 2. load of hay in: sabath day 22. heare came a warant for the deputies sabath day 20 and Tusday 31.

The sixt moneth is Agust and hath 31 days wensday the first my wife was at Clements Thursday the second I had in the whit pease and 273 oat sheaves and 305. 578. in all wensday the 8 we had all our wheate pease and oats into the Baren and wensday the 15 we made one Recke of hay the 16 day we received a leter from my Cosin wensday 22. a verie wet weeke ffriday our Children went to see Clement wensday 29. we made the second Reeke ffriday 31. The 27 Mr noyce went to the bay.

The seventh moneth is September & hath .30. day saterday the first Tusday I went to the bay being the 4 day Saterday the 8 day I was at Bostowne saterday the 15 I was at whome monday we got pales & satterday the 22. we got up pales The 20 day Thursday the Countie Courte was at new london Satterday 29. sabath day the 30 I was at nowig The first of october we did chuse deputies mr stanton was Chosen Sergant of the Traine band.

The eight moneth is october & hath 31 days monday the first the 2 day we was at new london the 3 & 4 day we made The list the 6 day I was wt lam but could not have my horse shewed monday The 8 & monday the 15 I brought up stakes for the sheep house the 16 day I had my horse shewed monday the 22 and sabath day the 28 mr noyce Taught after he came from The bay monday 29. I paid sha 2 bushells of Indean corne for philip tabor & made Even with sha Tusday 30 I made an end of all sider wensday 31 a day of Thanksgiving saterday 27 The Rams wer brought whome.

November is the ninth moneth & hat 30 days Thursday the first I was bound to Seaconck with the whit horse ffriday the 2d I delivered the horse to old Pains' wife at his house before mr william lord & daniell Smith the 3d I came home the 5 day we had A Towne meeting Thursday the 8 I was at new london the 9th day I was at mr Stantons about The list the 10th mr Richerson was heare for to See his list Thursday the 15. my wife was goeing to new london & came backe againe the 21 day I came from new london Thursday 22 the 30 day fell the snow it was ffriday.

The tenth moneth is december & hath 31 days Saterday the first The .6. day Sir Robert Car was at poquatuc I left my Commission with him the .5. day we Confirmed the agreement with mr noyce and signed it satterday the 8 day Thursday the 13 day mr Richerson came to my house to swear Aron Start Saterday the 15. monday the 17 day fell the Second snow & great Storme Saterday 22. the 3d snow Tusday 25 day & Xmas day wensday the 26. we met at the Captaines & Satterday .29. I made an End Threshing wheate monday the last of december I was at new london. I had 24£ of sugar of morgan.

The leventh moneth is Januarie & hath 31 days
Tusday the first wensday the .2. it snowed the 3d
great Snow Clement was heare Tusday the 8 we wer
at Tagwoncke the 9 day the meeting at mr Richersons Tusday 15 I was at Tagwonck Josepth cut his
finger the meeting at wheelers & Saterday the 19.
the 4 great snow I was at the Captaines & Tusday
22. 23 day 5 a greate snow storme I made an end of
our hemp we had the cubed horse in hand the 26 day
the .6. snow the 25 we wer all at Tagwonck I begun
threshing oats Tusday 29. Thursday 31. Ephraims
wife was sicke.

The Twelfth moneth is februarie & hath 28. days
friday the first Satterday the Second day & Candelmas day I made an End of Threshing of oats sabath
day I was not at meeting Tusday the .5. the meeting
is at my house: and ffriday the 8 I was at poquatuck
mill upon the Ice : friday 15. we had 44. bushells of
oats I was at meshuntucks with John denison saterday the 16. I begun the reek Witer brought the
canoow: monday 18 day agedouhet Toald us that the
Ketle was stolne as he heard: ffriday the 22. Sabath
24. the meeting was at mr Richersons monday 25.
hanah cow calved it was very wet: this winter was
much snow much deare was killed Tusday 26. day
the meeting was at the Captains Thursday the 28.

I was not well: the ffirst faier day we had in 10 weeks
Hermon garet (blurred) flagon.

The first month is march & hath 31 dayes & ffriday the first and is the yeare .1667. and from the
Creation .5616. & leap yeare: and The .19th yeare of
the reinge of our lord sovereing King Charles the
Secone: The 3 day and 4th we wer at new london the
8 day we wer at ffanings wensday the 13. the last
meeting at mr Richerdsons The 14 ffell a great snow.
ffriday the 15. ffriday 22. mr palmer & I agreed ffor
a barell of mallaces ffriday ye 29. our 4th Cow Calved
I made even with mr picket & Received a barell of
mallasses of mr palmer the 30 day I came whome it
was verie wet Sabath day 31. 27 mr Bruster was
heare

The second month is Aprill & hath 30 dayes monday the first monday the .8. I begun to plow in the
plaine & sow peas my wife was at poquanuck The
man was beaten at Tagwonck our black Cow Calved:
The 13 day I made an End of Sowing The Same day
the man was beaten mr denison was at my house and
p'pred the list.   Ephraim was heare monday the .15.
I rumeged the boxes The 19 day the Magestates was
at shas monday 22. mr denison his ffamilie was heare
The Captain was bound to the peace the 27 day being
Saterday I made an end of drawing Stons for the

seller: monday 29. we had a towne meeting to chuse depu(t)ies tusday 30

The third month is may & hath 31 days & wensday the first my wife was hurt with the horse by the pond The .6. day I was takeing The black mare with nathaniell lewis & wensday the 8. the 13 day I made an end of fenceing at the Creeke the 15 day wensday I & manaseth was in the woods 22 was wensday: I begun to wall the Seller saterday 25 day I made an End of laying the greate peeces of the Seller & I was with goodman Cheesbrough the same day Ephraim his daughter died and was Buried the 26 day & wensday 29. James measured 26 pole of wall and had Three pound &-1-10-0 the Same day I begun to cleave pales for the Celler: friday 31.

The ffouerth month is June and hath .30 days & saterday the first I brought pales for the new seller Saterday the 8. I ffetched Stones for the way into ye new seller ffriday the 14. brother Avery was heare saterday the .15. I was at lams with .10. pound of wool and satterday The 22 we begun to mow Jane Tould me of the Indean that was hanged: The 28 day being ffriday I set forth for Seconck with the Roane horse: The 27 day of this month my land at mooapeatke was laid out by James Averie and James morgan Sabath day the 30 I was at Seconck

The ffifte month is July & hath .31. days & monday
the first Tusday the 2 day I came from Seconck my
wife and hanah was at new london and monday the 8
day I and my wife and Josepth was at Averies the
10 day I sould Josepth his horse to mr Bull the 12
day I was at george geares and the 15 day being
monday and monday The .22. and vogie wet weather
saterday the .20 day I was at Crandals mill wensday
night 24th the great land fflood & monday 29 the 30
day tusday mr noyce received the Cow: and wensday
the 31. I sowed turneps

The sixt month is Agust & hath 31. days and
Thursday the first popiamut begun & wensday the .7.
I was at mr Stantons as I went to Crandalls & Thursday the .8. day saterday the 10. the ship was at
ffishers Iland: monday morning the .12. day was the
larum the Same day Brother Averie and sister was
heare and at tagwoncke: Tusday I was at lams: I had
10 loads of hay in the barne Thursday the .15. it was
voted at the Towne meeting that all the ffenced un-
broken lands should be listed at .5 s p: acker Thursday 22. The 2. shirts wer stolen 23. I made a reeck
of hay 24. I made .2. barels of sider Thursday 29.
10 M was heare lefftenant averie saterday 31.

The seventh month is september and hath 30. dayes
& sabath day the first and sabath day the .8. we wer

at norwhich: tusday the .10 we laid out the Indeans land morgan was with us The .12. day we viewed the Armes: & sabath day the 15. we wer at norwhich the Commissionors wer there the 18. day mr denison somonsd me to give Evidence at his house about an horse sabath day 22 monday 23 we prised mr noyce his Catell 24. brother Averie took the sheep the 28 day we was for the pres at quanandap sabath day 29.

my Estate to the Contrie list 170-10-00

The Eight month is october & hath .31. dayes and Tusday the first Tusday the 8 I went to Coneticut with mr stanton saterday the 19. I came whome Tusday 22. I went to Bostowne mr Bowster and with Catell that night we lay at willsons at the lead mines: it was the greate Thunder that killed 3 swine and a Calfe at narraganset Thursday morning between (harrise) and (Providence) I found A Ratten The monday after Captaine olliver gave me a leading rake

The ninth month is november & hath .30. days and ffriday the first I came whome from Bostowne Thursday the 7. day we made an End of carring of muck ffriday the 8 day The 7 day Thurday my wife fell of her mare and hurt her selfe verie much Tusday the 12 I went to mr Bewsters ffriday the 15 the first snow fell I came whome from laying out land

Clement was heare ffriday 22 monday we met about the mill I caried a bushell of Corne to badcoks for willson the 27 I sowed hemp being wensday saterday the 30.

The tenth month is december and hath .31. days sabath day the first wensday the 4th it snowed the 4th snow saterday the 7th gerson & his wife was heare sabath day the 8. and 9 day we Killed the swine The 10 day we mended the Chimbly the 11 day it was wet sabath day the 15. the .17. day I was at new london ffor Sugar The 20 & 21. days we made the orchard hedge sabath day 22. The 28 day I borowed five bushels of Indean Corne of mr picket I sent a leter to barbades by Simon grover sabath day 29 Tusday 31.

The leventh month is Januarie & hath .31. dayes and wensday the first I fecthed whome the bay mare a littel white spot on the forehead & one white ffoot and a white streake crost the top of the nose from nostrill to nostrill the 3 day manaseth fecthed his Cow: the six day the seller fell downe wensday the Eight I broke my ax the 9 day A Towne meeting the 14 day W(e) made mr noyce his rate wensday the 15. John badcoke brought Two paier of shews we had 2 lams wensday the 22 mr noyce was heare and had the Rate delivered the 21 day moser and hanah huet was with mr noyce wensday the 29 ffriday manaseth land was laid out 31 day.

The twelfth month is ffebruarie & hath .29. dayes: this ends the leap yeare and satterday the ffirst monday the 3 day I was with the Captaine saterday the .8. day it was wet and the 11 and 12 days we had a towne meeting satterday the 15 I begun to prune my Trees it was wet the week ffollowing I pruned Trees and saterday the 22. Tusday 25. I paid mr picket mr palmer and Joshua Raymond and sould The Tanner 19 shilling worth of oyle: Thursday 27 day I made an end of pruning of Trees Tho 26 day we saw the blase 28 I was to go to badcocks saterday 29.

The ffirst month is march & hath .31. d: sabath day the first and in the first after the leap yeare and from the Creation .5617. and the yeare .1668. and the 20th yeare of the reinge of our lord King Charels the second the .6. day Thomas Tracie and leaffing- well was heare the .7. dai I branded .2. Coults I sowed hemp & pease in the orchard sabath day the .8. day: sabath day the 15. The 13. I was at mr palmes I had A barell of mallases wensday the 18. we made an End between Jossepth & Marie Averie monday the 30 day I ffecthed my wifes mare and 26. day Thursday we trained fryday .31.

The second moneth is Aprile and hath 30 days

wensday the ffirst we sowed pease in the plaine &
wheate: the 7. day we had a towne meeting wensday
the .8 I gardned the .9 day I mended the Brige &
was at Tagwoncke The 14. day it snowed and the 15
day being wensday ye 16 day we plowed ffor sega-
moot in the plaine The 20 day mr Brewster and mr
star was heare I marked the red mares Coult wensday the .22. I sowed fflax the 23 I was with mr noyce
to pay him it was wet.

The 29 of Agust mr noyce taught and the third
day of october not since till 1667

The third moneth is may and hath .31. days ffriday the first Thursday I was at black hall John came
hither ffriday the 8. the .11. day I was at norig and
burnt my bill: the 12. day John went Away I was to
goe to the Court the 14 day was the Electun ffriday
the 15 The 17 day I was sicke the 22 I was at Courte
the being ffriday monday 25 I came whome the 30
day I paid thee firkin of buter to badcok sabath
day 31.

The 22 of June 1668 Ephraim his son was borne.

The fouerth moneth is June and hath .30. days
monday the ffirst: The .4. I came from new london
the same day I received .3 letters ffrom bristoll &
monday the 8 I was caring wood the tenth I was

lookeing horses Monday the .15 hanah went to Tag-wonck The same day was a towne meeting to Chuse a Constable Thomas wheeler was Chosen my lot drawne and the 18 day we ended all about our ffarmes agedowset his five ackers laid out and he and I exchanged monday 22. the 23 day I was branding horses 24 day my wife came whome sicke ffrom Tag-wouncke monday 29 I had mowed most of my orchard Tusday the 30 I was to go to New london we Killed the catle.

July is the fift moneth and hath .31. days wensday the first Thursday mr hill was maried the second day wensday the 8. I was at Crandals mill ffriday the .10. we had our ffloore laid I had ffouer loads and halfe of hay in the baren wee wer (sentence unfinished) Tus-day the 14 Cap denison nehemiah palmer & Tho minor was Chosen to make the Contrie Rate and lists the 15 day we made the Contrie Rate being wens-day the 17 day I was at pocatuck the 20 day mon-day Josepth had Twentie six shillings of wamppum and wensday the 22. 23 I had 2 load of pease into the barne the .25 day saterday we had all our oates & pease into the barne Rachell mason was heare wens-day 29. Tho bell came to worke my wheat came all downe ffriday 31 I was at badcoks

The sixt moneth is Agust and hath .31. days sat-

terday the ffirst we tooke all our fflag out of the
water the ffifte day wensday I was at Crandals mill
saterday the .8. Crandall and his wife was heare we
had Ten load of hay whome monday 10 day I went to
bostowne with the oxen saterday the 15 monday the
17 I came whom from bostowne and saterday 22 I
ffecthed the litel Reeck with the .2. steer: and The
.27. we had ale our hay whome .28. we gathered
aples saterday .29. I writ letters to Bristoll monday
31.

The seventh moneth is september and hath .30.
days Tusday the ffirst saterday the .5. we set up the
place for to put corn in monday the 7 we gathered
hops Tusday the 8 Thomas perke was heare The 11
I was at new london monday the 14 the Towne meeting about parkers land Tusday the 15. the 17 day I
was at the Courte saterday I came whome Tusday
.22. the Jurie was discharged Thursday the 24 was
our Traing day: .36. was ffined when we came to the
Top of the greate hill we met Thomas perk and his
sonn Thomas perk and Robert holmes it Rained and
wensday the 30 we made an End of carring of indean
corne

The Eight moneth is october and hath .31. days
Thursday the ffirst the secon day wee chose deputees
p'fected our list: mr Richerdson discovered Captaine

gookin his horse the .8. day John his wife and Children was heare my wife and I was at london and let the Catele to John keny Thursday the .15 ffriday the 16 John & the Rest went away The 7 day of this moneth John ffish was hurt and Thursday The 22. I made an End of Shuflin in the yard the .18 day mr Thorneton Taught heare thursday .29. we wer to traine

The ninth moneth is november and hath .30. days and sabath day the ffirst The 4 day we delivered the mares to nathaniell Cooper sabath day the .8. mr noyce came whome the 9 day I sent to John and sabath day the 15 the 16 day we broke our wheel Caring muck the 17 day we gathered Turneps we had bushels wensday the 18 was A day of Thanksgiving sabath day 22 the high Tide was sabath 29 mr noyce apoynted the 30 day of december to be a day of ffasting and debate being wensday month and munday the 30 day we laid out 300 ackers of land ministrie

The tenth moneth is december and hath .31. days Tusday the ffirst we laid out 200 ackers of land for the ministry The third day the .2. snow and Elisha Cheesbroughs son was borne the 6 day my wife ffell of the mare at the Cart brige the 7 day we looked land the 8 day Tusday I was at the Captaines and gallops the 15 day tusday the 3. snow I begun to thresh and wensday the 4 snow my sons went to new london Tusday the .22. I was at new london Thursday .24. I arested shumatuck 26 day williams was heare

The 16 day of November 1669 Thomas park Junior ffetched a barell of sider and one bushell of apples that was the Just sume ffor the house building

The leventh moneth is Januarie and hath .31. days ffriday the ffirst and ffriday the eight I tooke up my bay horse The 13 day mr noyce Captaine and his wife was heare the 14 day Ephraim and marie was heare and ffecthed wood the ffifteen ffriday The 20 day wensday The meeting was at our house ffriday 22 The snow melted all away the 23 day we ffecthed wood ffriday the 29 and sabath the .31.

The 25 day of ffebruarie .1668. there was due to me Thirteen shillings from Thomas bell.

The Twelvth moneth is ffebruary & hath .28. days monday the ffirst: this is the yeare of our lord god .1668. from the Creation .5617. and the first after the leap yeare: and The .20th yeare of the Reinge of king Charles the second the .2. day a towne meeting about mr Richarson building upon marshall wights land the same day I was Chosen Towne Treasurer the third day I was at london and paid the marshall the 8 day monday we wer laing out an acker of land at beaporton the ninth day we sent .4. gallons of oyle to goodwife Cheesbrough the 15 day I was with mr noyce at london monday 22 the 24 I was at poquatuck with mr noyce The 25 day Thursday mr Richardson cried out murther The 27 day I was at new london sabath day 28

The ffirst moneth is march and hath 31. dayes monday the ffirst and is the yeare .1669. and the second from the leap yeare and ffrom the Creation .5618. and the .21. yeare of the reing of our lord king Charels the second the first day I was with my wife at Ephraims the 2 day our towne Constable was arested with others ffriday the ffift day we made the Contrie Rate mond(ay) the 8 day mr Richardson brought me my almineck the 10 day I ffetched my Carte wheels monday .22. it was snow & williams was heare the last Cow Claved I read mr damfforts letter The 31 day wensday the meeting was at my house mr stanton goodman wheeler nathaniell Cheesbrough nehemiah palmer John gallop senior goodman serels Josia witerall wer satisfied so to joyne togeather

The second moneth is Aprile and hath 30 dayes Thursday the ffirst manaseh and will begun at the ffarme Thursday The .8 we lined the house the .9. we Threshed the 10 bushells of Corne Thursday the 15

wee met at the meeting house and .13 or 14 gave in
their nams to begin a Church and Thursday 22 my
wife was at Tagwonck Joseph was heare & william
more I had sowed my wheate saterday the 24 day I
made an End of soweing in the plaine Thursday The
29. mr samuell mason Chosen leeftenant ffriday 30

The Third moneth is may and hath .31. days saterday the ffirst the third day I made an End of plowing
and sowd hemp and saterday the 8 day and saterday
the 15 day I was ffecthing of hedging stuff the 16
day I was Taken lame at the meeting at new london
saterday 22. I delivered 2 bushelles of Corne to
Thomas wheeler munday 24 I ffecthed whom the
Table The 29 day being saterday I set up my gate by
my house monday 31

The 30 day of June .1669. I had the A p bation of
the Church of new london to p'take with the Church
of norwhich.

The fouerth moneth is June and hath 30 day tusday the first the 2 day the Court begun that Court I
maried huntley and marie barens Tusday the .8 day
I was lookeing Cat ffriday the .11. day Clement and
his wife and Children was heare we tooke up Cat monday the 14 day we set fforth ffor Bostowne wensday
the 16 I sould my horses to page satterday the 19 I

came whome Tusday the 22 I had my hay out of the orchard Tusday 29. wensday The 30 I was at new london and had Testimony ffrom the Church ffor me and my wife being owned to be under their watch.

July is the ffift moneth and hath 31 days Thursday the ffirst and monday the 5 mr ffich mr Brewster was heare monday the 5 Thursday the .8 day and Thursday the .15. & Thursday .22 I was at Tagwonnck it was the day after the marshall did goe away after the Examination of ninicrat The 28 day wensday a meeting of the Select men we had our white pease

The .12th. of Agust .1669. being Thursday leeftenant Averie and his wife with parte of his ffamilie was heare

The sixt moneth is August and hath .31. days sabath day the ffust the 4th day is wensday we went with the govenor That night was the storme sabath day the 3. Tusday the 10 day I was at mr palmes wensday the .11. the meeting was at the widow palmers and sabath day the .15. Thursday The 19 the Towne meeting sabath day The 22 Tusday 24 I was at badcoks to have my horse shewed and bought ffouer Barels of the Cooper ffor a barel of sider The 30th day I was at the ffarme and layd out two ackers of land to be broken by agedouset there was a meeting

at benits house .31. day tusday I gathered hops goodwife ffaning was heare with lillie

The seventh moneth is september and hath .30.
days the ffirst wensday The meeting was at my house
sabath day the .5 mr noyce was sicke wensday the 8
day I was at meshuntucks to agree with the Indeans.
Robert fflemen was heare at worke wensday the .15.
there should have been a Courte at new london
the .16. day being the third Thursday In spetember
The .19. day Joseph his sonn was borne 22. wensday
I had a ster I came ffrom mr hills at new london with
nayls my second ffit with the ffever

The 12 day of october mr noyce went into the bay
3d of october he taught

October is the Eight moneth and hath .31. days
ffriday the ffirst and ffriday The .8. we prest Sider the
9th day samuell was gathering Chestnuts Ephraims
Sonn was broken The 10th day sabath Master noyce
was ile and came not to the meeting house ffriday I
made a end of gathering of apells it was the 15 day
ffriday 22 the 23 The Canoow went to new london
with Corue sabath 24 marie minor was taken sick
Tusday 26. ther fell a greate snow wensday 27. we
killed the Cow ffriday the 29 sabath day .31. we had
no meeting monday the ffirst of november 1669 samuell saw the geldin at meshuntucks

The niuth month is november and hath .30. days
the ffirst monday samuell had 3 bushell of Corne at
meshuntucks wensday the third I was at mill monday
the 8 Tusday .9. a day of Thanksgiving mother
palmer was heare monday the .16. Ephraim his wife
and Child was heare it was wet the messengers was
to go to the Court mr noyce came ffrom the bay the
.6. day of this month Thursday the .18. day my wife
was taken verie ill the second snow fell we made an
End of Carring of muck and ffecthed wood and monday .29. Joseph was heare Tusday 30 we Carrid wood

The tenth moneth is december and hath .31. days
the ffirst wensday the .8. day the (blotted out) met
about the cloths that was ffound the .9. day being
Thursday the 3d snow fell The 13 day munday manaseth went to new london the 14 day we made a brige
at mistusuck the 16 day Thursday the Constable
apoynted the publishing of the orders to the Indeans
ffriday the .17. Ephraim .2d. son was borne 21 day
4th snow ffell wensday 22 I was at Badcoks wensday .29. I was at Crandals mill we had .7. snows
ffriday 31 we wer Ending the busines at quaqutage

The leventh moneth is Januarie and hath .31. days
the ffirst day is satterday this week the .8. snow ffell
Clement and manaseth was heare and saterday the
.8. I received a letter ffrom mr witherell saterday the

15 we had .9. snows I copid the leter to the bay hauah was at Ephraim his house the 17 day the 10th snow the 18. day Tusday I went to Badcoks we had one calf & lambs the 21 day the .11 snow fell the swine wer to be Driven away saterday the 22. day the 12 snow ffell, wheeler was heare and had 4 orders written out burnt 1 we had 4 Calves the 28 day we had 15 snows I made an end of Threshing of white peas satterday the 29 day the 30 day we had 17 snows monday the 31.

The twelvth moneth is ffebruarie & hath .28. days the ffirst is Tusday saterday the .5. the .20. snow ffell I was at samuell Cheesbroughs and had 16 pound of fflax and at ffanings to speake with morgan: Tusday the .8. I comed fflax Josepth and mary was heare satterday the 12 the 22 snow ffell The 15 day tusday I was at new london the day of humiliation the 23 snow ffell ffriday the 18 day James Averie was married wensday 23 the meeting was at mother palmers and That night ffell the 24. snow thursday 24 it rained.

we have had 26 snows the ffirst week in march

The ffirst month is march and hath .31. days Tusday the ffirst: and is the yeare of the lord 1670. and the third yeare after the leape yeare and ffrom the Creation .5619 and the 23. yeare of the reing of our lord King Charles the second and Tusday the .8. we met at Elisha Cheesbroughs ffriday the .11. we begun to plow it snowed all day Tusday the .15. it snowed Tusday the 22 it snowed goodman prentice and Nathaniel lewis was heare I branded horses at Elishas Tusday the 29. I made an End of sowing it snowed the .27. manaseh was heare The .30. day was to be a day of humiliation Thursday the .31.

The ffirst wensday in aprill was a publick ffast

The second moneth is Aprill and hath .30. days ffriday the ffirst ffriday the .8. we made the Contrie and mr noyce his Rate the .9. day I payd my Contrie Rate to mr stanton ffriday the .15. our white backed heighfer Calved the .16. day we wer at the Iland ffor hop poles the 13. & 14 days I was diging stones at the ffarme ffor my Chimbly the 16 day serls brought whome the lining Cloth ffriday .22. I weeded the hops I lent my Canoow to the Irishman saterday The .23. I was .62. years ould: I had news that the ould man would have all the Corne at the ffarme Thursday .28. sam came whome Il from new london ffriday .29. it was wet and satterday the .30. Tusday the .26. of this month Joseph morgan and doritie Park was maried.

The .29. day william Chapman demanded of me 01-01-06 ffor Jerimie Adams.

The third moneth is may and hath .31. days The
ffirst is sabath day: the 5 day I was at The ffarme and
Ephraim with me ffryday The 6. I was planting Corne
in the playne The .7th day manaseth and James
Averie Came heare sabath day the .8. mr noyce said
he must goe abroad I put up a paper on the meeting
house doore the 10. day the Two mares ffolled: the
12 day I made an end of plowing the 14. day I Ended
the litle house sabath day the 15. and sabath day
the .22. I was com ffrom stratford monday 23. I covered the oven and sabath day 29. The .27. day I was
at new London hanah and marie with their Children
came whome with me monday 30. we sheered our
sheep Tusday 31. The 25. day wensday the Leeftenant
tooke the Charge of the Company in the ffield.

The ffourth moneth June and hath .30. days the
ffirst is wensday: and wensday the 8 I was at the
County Court and Tusday the 14 I was at badcoks
and there was Tho stanton Junior: and wensday the
.15. the Court at new London about the Roade Island
people the 17 day ffriday I was sent ffor to com to
the Com'r's at mr Richardsons house the same day
and the 18 day Both we wer at poquatucke and
Tooke 3 prisnors monday the 20 I was at badcoks the
majestrats wer gon to the naragansets and we begun
to mow in the orchard wensday 22 leeftenant mason

brought whome his wife we begun to make hay the majestrats wer at naraganset 23. we brought the majestrates to misticke saterday 25. we got sume hay into the barne wensday 29. thursday 30. James and Abram Ended mowing by the Creeck.

The fift moneth is July and hath .31. days The ffirst is ffriday: tusday the 5 the Comitee met Thursday the .7. we rune the Est line ffriday the .8. I sowed turneps in the litle ochard The 14 day Thursday we wer at mr stautons about walter house being murthered ffriday the 15 mr noyce his note came to me and I caried it to Captaine denison monday the 18 the Commitee met at mr Richardsons thursday 21. mr Crandale was heare I had in fouer loads of oats the 22. day ffriday I was at mr samuell Cheesbrough house mr stanton Came not: and 27 day I and my wife was at new london goodman Rice & william Hoase was received in to the Church ffriday .29. I was caring stones ffor mr noyce I had all my English corne into the barne sabath day .31.

The 2 day of Agust 1670. Crandals wife was buried

The sixt moneth is Agust and hath .31. days the ffirst is monday: the ffirst and second I was at narraganset with mr stanton wensday the third day we plowed in the plaine the .8. day monday the day after the storme: Thursday the 11 we Came whome with

wilson and mumford the 16 day Tusday mr stanton
was heare wensday the 17 I was with mr samuell
Cheesbrough he and his daughter Abygale was sicke
Thursday the 18 day we wer to Rayse our house at
the ffarme and did it satterday the 20. we made our
second Reeck hanah had her ffirst ffit and The ninth
day with samuell wile be ffriday the 26. day monday
.22. we agreed with wheeler and gallop senior to pay
mr Hill 4-15-0 monday 29 we met at samuel Cheesbroughs mr Richardson was goeing to the bay wensday 31. the meeting was at our hous: the 28 day
Clement was heare it was the sabath.

The seventh moneth is september and hath .30.
days the ffirst is Thursday: our Brother Elisha Cheesbrough departed this life in the fforenoone monday the
.5. I was at mr stantons about the Cou(n)try busines
our brother garshoms wife was delivered of a young
daughter Thursday the .8. I gathered the hops
Thursday the 15 and thursday the 22 I was at Court
monday the .26. manaseth was maried.

wensday the .16. of november 1670 we had a day
of Thankesgiveing.

Tusday the .27. of december .1670. I branded a
horse Coult ffor hanah he was blacke with: Ʇ: on the
ffur shoulder and cut a halpenie on Each Eare and
cut of his taile by the stumpe.

The Eight month is october and hath .31. days the
ffirst is satterday: the ffift day mr broadstreet was
ordayned the 7th day I went in to the bay the 14 day
I came whome and saterday the .15. monday 17 I
ffetched whome samuell his Cows tusday and wensday we sowed Rye and thursday ffryday 21 I was at
new London saterday .22. I sowed wheat in the plaine.

The .21. of december .1670. was a day of humilliation Through the Colony of Coneticut Tusday the .27.
of december .1670 I branded a blacke horse Coult on
the ffur shoulder with : T : and Cut an halpenie on
Each eare for hanah.

The ninth moneth is november and hath .30. days
The ffirst is Tusday: The Court was That week Tusday the .8. the .9. day we killed the swine the .10
day we wer at new London the .11. day ffriday we
killed the other swine Tusday the 15. we had a Towne
meeting Thursday 17 we had a meeting to Inventarie
Elishas Lands the 18 and 19 days we Caried muck
out of the yard Tusday 22. John gallop and his wife
was heare and ffrancis was heare the Indean Tusday
29. we met at mr Richardsons wensday The 30 we
had a towne meeting snow.

The Tenth moneth december and hath .31. days
The ffirst is Thursday: I was at the ffarme and Caried
the doore the ffirst snow ffell wensday the 7th heare

was a Courte and the 8 the Court was Ended the .9th day I threshed wheate the 15 day Thursday the Committee met at mr Richardsons and Thursday the 22 I Caried the last of goodman Searles his Corne .13. bushels: of which he oweth -1-1-0 The 29. of december being Thursday the Committee met at mr stantons saterday the .31. packer was heare and had A firckin of sider and halfe a bushell of gray pease.

The .10. day of Januarie 1670. the Court about Crandall and lewis was at mr stantons house.

The leventh moneth is Januarie and hath .31. days The ffirst is Sabath day my wife Tooke phisicke Josephs wife and Child was heare sabath day the .8. mr Noyce warned a meeting at mother palmers on wensday com seven night and sabath day the .15. wa(s) the ffirst sacrament of the lords supper administred by mr broadstreet daniell Stebbins was baptised: sabath day .22. monday .23. I made Even with Robert ffleman: the .21. I made an End of Threshing of oats sabath day .29. Tusday the 31. I was at the ffarme with John Ascrat and his wife

the third day of march .1670. .71. John Ascrat went to the farme to live.

The .21. march I sent to John

The twelvth moneth is ffebruarie and hath .28.

days The ffirst is wensday: I made agreement with
John Ascraft about the ffarme and wensday the .8.
the meeting was at our hous Tusday the .14. Poquia-
nuts mother had ffifie shillings to pay In ffencing
wensday the 15. it snowed thursday the 16. we run
the Line ffrom mistick to poquatucke ffouer miles
three quarters and Twentie Rod monday the 27 and
Tusday .28. Clement was heare

The 10. 11. 12. 13. and 14. of march 1670. 71 I
made hedg at the Creeck.

The 14 of Agust 1671. John Ascrate son was borne
it being monday as I was Informed

The ffirst moneth is march and hath .31. days: it is
leap yeare and is the yeare of the lord .1671. and
ffrom the Creation .5620. and the .23. yeare of the
Reigne of our Lord King Charles the second: and
wensday is the first day: a meeting at mother palmers
Thursday the second we had a Towne meeting saterday the .4th. I made an End of pruninge the orchard
manaseth was heare Wensday The 8. good(man)
parker Calked the Canoow. I made an End of the
orchard fence wensday the .15. we fecthed Armestrong
and Wilcoxs the 16. & 17. days we wer at mr Richardsons the 18. day we sowed oats the 22 being wensday the meeting was heare the .27. John denisons

second son was borne heare should have been a towne meeting wensday .29. I sowed pasneps: friday .31.

The second moneth is Aprile and hath .30. days the ffirst day is saterday: and the .8. day saterday we wer Laying out Land at the Est side poquatuck River tusday the .11. I made an End of plowing in the playne. Joseph and I rune the head Lyne: saterday the 15 I was at Tagwoncke Tusday the 18 day Abram and Secanoot made an End of the log fence the 19 day wensday I had a note from mr stanton: tho .20. day thursday Ephraims daughter was borne friday 21. I ended the hedg by the gate saterday .22. and saterday the .29. we had the young bay mare had a sorel mare Coult with ffouer white ffeet and white streake down the forehead thus : ҫ : Eare marked with a halpenie on the fore side of Each Eare: sabath day the .30.

The third moneth is may and hath .31. days the ffirst day is monday I was at Tagwoncke at gallops at mill: Thursday the fouerth our Canoow was adrift the 3d. we wer at new London our mallaces came whome Saterday the 6. the Comitee should have met the day. The white faced mare had a white faced horse Coult he (had) fouer white feet and a halpeny Cut on Each Eare & a wald eye munday the 15. my wife an hanah was at new London. I wrot to John and went to mill monday 22 samuell fecthed the Bees our Cart wheel was broken thursday .25. we planted Corne not a peke my wife had a fit of ague saterday 27 mr noyce and Tho: bell brought my gray mare and Coly whome sabath .28. the sacrament was at new london munday .29. the Towne meeting weusday 31. we wer at Crandalls and sanders to serve Summons.

The ffouerth moneth June and hath .30 days the ffirst is Thursday goodman wheeler fecthed a Copie of the Towne order respecting the land in difference his daughter sarah was maryed: Thursday the 8 we made an End weeding the 9th Leeftenant smith was heare the 10th we planted Cabeg plants Thursday the 15. mr Brewster was heare I was at babcocks the Trayne company met and Thursday 22. I cleared lands at the farme friday I Came whome and went to see the Leeftenant he was gone to Norrige

The .26. Clement and his wife and Children was heare the 30 day friday the Select Men weiwed the Ministry Land Concerning where to set the Meeting House it was the last may and fryday.

Monday the 14. of Augst 1671 The Rams wer Caried to goosbery Island.

The fift moneth is July and hath .31. days the ffirst is saterday we Ended Hilling in the Little orchard:

Jaqueneg and his Wife to be reconsiled the .7th. day
we wer five a hilling and we had the Hay out of the
orchard the .8. day saterday the bottom was mowed
Enos had the greate Conoow The .10th. a towne meeting the .13th. Bouls was maried the .14th we made
an End of Hilling the .15. day saterday at night
Mother palmer departed this Life saterday the .22. I
had three loade of white pease and Two Loades of
oates In to the barne and saterday the .29. it was wet
monday 31. The 24 day wensday samuell was at
Crandals mill::

sabath day the sixt of Agust the sacrament was
Administred at new London

The sixt moneth is Agust and hath .31. days the
ffirst is Tusday Clement & manaseth was heare I had
made an End Cuting of Rie and Tusday the .8. I was
at plow in the pease ground Tusday the .15 my wife
and hanah was at new London we Cleared the Hay
out of the Low bottoms the .17. day Thursday mr
stanton Captayn winthroup John g(a)llop senior and
I was with the Indeans to publish the Court Order.
John morgan was heare to trim the sider barels .2.
days the .23. day my wife and hanah was at Tagwonck and brought Litle Ephraim it being wensday
the 24th. day Thursday the Towne meeting was to

bring in the Lists Tusday .29. thursday .31. we had all our Hay whome that Abram and James Cut

The Seventh moneth is september and hath .30. days the ffirst ffriday we gathered hops: the 2d. deliverance blackman was heare to tell me that he would goe to stratford the 4th. of this month we agreed with John ascrafte to Leave the farm Emund faning Tho: park Joseph Morgan Joshua holmes witnesses mouday the 11th. the Comitee met at Mr Richardsons ffriday the 15 I was at new London monday the .18. the Comitee was at Master Richardsons Tusday the .19. goodwife witer was Lost The .11. day the broayl was at poquatucke ffriday .22. 23 day I had all my Corne in sabath day 24. I had a letter from my Cousin ffriday 29. I made the last hay Reecke Clement was heare: saterday the 30. wee sowed the acker of wheate.

The Eight moneth is october and hath .31. days the ffirst is sabath day this sixth day we made an End of sowing of wheate and Joseph daughter was Borne: I delivered my horse to mr Leverit and went to Tagwoncke sabath day the .8. this weeke mr noyce went into the Bay and sabath day the .15. the .17th. I sowed Rie samuell was at Towne the 20 and .21. I was at the farme the 22 is sabath day the .23. I made Even with John morgan and payd him 4 bushells of

Corne and an halfe the 24th day tusday I made the writings between hudson leverit and my selfe sabath day the .29. monday the .30. I set forth for the bay: Tusday .31. our sons John Clement and the rest was heare.

The ninth moneth is november and hath .30. days the ffirst is wensday wensday the .8. we came from the bay and killed the steers and the great hogg wensday the 15 a day of thankesgiveing at new London the 20 & 21. we Caried muck and wensday .22. Thursday .23. my wife was at new London there fell the second snow: Hanah was taken ile: we made Even with mr Raymond and one peny Credit when my wife had taken: 9 lbs of Coton woole monday 27. mr parkers Katch was com: wensday 29 a thanks-giveing thursday 30.

The tenth month is december and hath .31. days the ffirst is ffriday Tusday the .5. heare was a Court wensday the sixt I was at new london ffriday the .8. it was foule weather I went to mr Richardsons: and samuell at the farme The .10. day the sacrament was administred at new London friday the 15. we apoynted a place for the meeting house the 16 day saterday I begun to Thresh wheate the 18 day monday it snowed friday 22 we met at mr Richardsons tusday 26. the Comitee met at mr stantons the 27 wensday we the

select men wer at quaquatage about the Child that
was murthered mr stanton tould me that he was goeing
to marie hanah Huit The .29. day friday we sen(t)
to Hartford the murtherer saterday .30. sabath day
.31.

The leventh moneth is Januarie and hath .31. days
the ffirst is monday Tusday the .2. I was at new
london the 3 day a meeting at our Brother moses:
monday the .8. the 9th day a Towne meeting to let
out the meeting house to Build The .15. day monday
we wer about the Indeans the same day samuell went
to the farme the 16. day Abram Cut wood my wife
went to Searles fridat the .19. I was at mr stantons
to send the Indeans to Hartford to p'cecut Mowdam
for murther: the voyolent Could begun monday .22.
wensday 24 the meeting was heare satterday 27. the
greate drift of snow samuell was at the farme monday
.29. wensday .31. samuell went to the farme: sabath
day 28 there was no meeting.

The .12th. moneth is ffebruarie and hath .29. days
the ffirst day is Thursday and thursday the .8. we had
marked the swine at the farme thus S: and came to
good(man) wheelers about the Ridglen the .9th. day
Emund was heare wensday the .14 I my wife was at
the farme and goodwife ffaning Thursday the .15.
mr Richardson his barne was Raysed monday the .12.

day the Constable gershum and James yorke was heare to have a stray mare Recorded sabath day the 18. the sacrament was administred mr noyce was there Thursday .22. it was wet I had made an End threshing of pease: we had three Calves Thursday .29. the day of Election.

the .30. day of July being wensday york was surrendered to the duch

An Allmenack for the yeare of our Lord: 1672 from the Creation 5621. and the first yeare after the Leap yeare and the .24. of the reigne of our Lord King Charles the second: march is the first moneth and hath 31. days friday the first Thursday the .7th. we made the Contrie Rate and mended the Cart bridge mr noyce was heare and Joseph his wife and Children friday the .8. my Wife tooke phisicke tusday the .12. goodman dart was heare wensday the .13. the meeting was at Moses palmers Thursday the .14. I shewed John Lewis his lot friday the .15. a meeting at mr Richardsons about the meeting house the .18. day of This moneth we Run the line from Weakapoug to misticke friday 22 I begun to sow wheate the 25 I sowed wheate friday .29. sabath day 31 mr noyce Taught out of the .12. Chapter of the Revelations and the .9th. vers:

The second moneth is Aprile and hath .30. days

monday the first we made the hedge at the watters
side Tusday the .2. I was at mr stantons about his
Indean Jeane wensday the 3d the meeting was at our
house monday the Eight: tusday the .9th I was with
Deacon parke Captaine denison did bring hither five
pounds of fflax the 10th day deacon parke and we
wer at quaquatage the 11 day mr noyce and deacon
parke & the Company was heare I agreed with mr
noyce and Tho: park: the .15th day monday we met
at mr Richardsons Ralph parke came in the 17 day I
was at new London monday .22. we wer at mr Richardsons wensday wee met at mr Samuel Cheesbro
being .24. Thursday .25. there was a trayneng mis-
tucksuck Tusday the .30. wee Chose deputies. Clement
and manaseth wives wer heare the same dav manaseth bay mare came whome againe

The third moneth is may and hat(h) .31. days
weusday the first: sabath day the .5. there was a sacrament at new London monday and Tusday I and my
wife was at the farme & wensday the .8. wee Covered the Seller and wensday the .15. the Church at
new London met. nathaniell Cheesbrough was ill the
.16. day the Catle was to goe (to) the farme tusday
.21. the doctor let Nathaniell Cheesbroughs blood.
mr parker had the oats aboard .40. bushells to bring
me Two barels of mallasses: wensday .22. wee made

hedge upon the wall: wensday .29. I and my Three sonns Clement Ephraim and manaseth was at stratford the 30th A day of humilliation friday .31. 22. Catle at the farme: the 16 day of may the first of June .1672. coming from stratford I fayled in takeing a Cup of Sider to much to the greaving of my sons Clement Ephraim & manaseth.

The fouerth moneth is June and hath .30. days saterday the first: Tusday the .4th. I came whome I had my horse shewed at Lams: saterday the .8. I was at mill samuell fecthed munchapeg the Committee met at new London the 12 and 13. I was at poquanump: the 15. saterday the 16. the majestrates wer hears the 17. wee plowed in the playne the .18. wee wer at the farme mr noyce was heare H. G. was maried: satterday 22. Cleaveing pales the .24. and midsumur day I was at mill and at mr Richardsons &· Joseph was hears the .26. and the .27. day we fecthed our mallaces from mr parker wee tooke up goods ate Raymonde to the value of A. 11£. 02s. 09p. and payd a firkin of butter to mr Hill: one pound .11. shillings saterday the .29. I was at Rebeckahs to geet mr balden: sabath day the .30. Clement and marie was heare

The 13th of Agust 1672. wee Caried Away the Rams to the Island.

The fift moneth is July and hath .31. days the first is monday: the .2. day the Commitee met with squm-acut people the .3. day I and my wife was at the farme the .5. day we were at Ephraims house the whole Towne: monday the .8. I was at new London the 10th. day my wife and I was with mr stanton the 12th day I was at the farme the .14th day the sacra-ment was the .15 day monday wee put the wheels to the Cart that Clement made us the .18. day friday: Hanah steerie was delivered the .20. we Rept our Rye the .22. we wer Cuting of oats and fecthing in the sumer wheat and pease: monday the 29. wee Cut winter wheat wensday .31. wee made an End of Reap-ing.

Roger Steerie said that he went in to the bay the .12. day of september .1671. & sume say he stayed .5. weeks:

The sixt moneth is Agust and hath .31. days Thursday the first: saterday the third I had all the English Corne with into the house Clement & mana-seth went home monday the .5. I fecthed whome the meate Abram began to mowe my Wife was at new London there was a Court at mr stantons the .7th. day wensday Elizabeth Witter was buried wee wer at plowin of the playne I and my Wife was at Ed-mund ffanings Thursday the .8. I was a thresh-

ing wheate: the 12. day was the EClips wee had our
oxen to the farme the 14th. my Wife was at fanings
wee Layd out 20. Ackers of Land for the smith The
oxen Came from the farme: Thursday the .15. wee
made Hay & fecthed .2. Loads of wood thursday .20.
wee wer at Rebekah house wensday wee Came to new
London to mr Broadstreets Thursday .22. wee came
whome: we had .2. paier of shews the butter weighed
.73. Thursday .29. wee had 17. loads of Hay whome:
samuell plowed the first acker for wheate I was Lame:
saterday .31. The .29. Agust I sowed wheate

The seventh moneth is september and hath .30.
days sabath day the first: the .2. day I fetched the
Calves from the farme the .6. day I made an End of
soweing wheate the .5. day I Rod About mr noyce his
Rate sabath day .8. monday .9. wee had the hay by
the Creecke stacked wee wer about sam Colver and
matha fish 10. 11. & 12th we were upon the same
Account wee sent samuell Colver to goale we traced
the Indean Corne & made one barel of sider: the .19.
day is Thursday I came from the Court.

the .7. of october .1672. An mason was maried

Carie Lathams acount for the yeare 1672 .24th.
october
†††††††††††††††††††††††††††††††††

The .30th. of october .1672. mr stanton sayd he had maried Tho: Brand:

The Eight moneth is october and hath .31. days tusday the first: the 2 day I was at mr stantons about Indean busines yt night goodwife burrows died the 3 & 4th day we mended the chimbley the .5th. I fecthed shovels I had a paier of horse shews of John denison it being saterday the .8 day I went to the Court the .19. day I came whome: the 31. one day is apoynted to be a day of Thanksgiveing The .29. & the 30. days I fecthed pales the 24 day I Reckned with Carie there was .3 due me the 30 day the Carpenters fecthed their Tools with our Canoow & my wife was at new london.

The ninth moneth is november and hath .30. days friday the first: the .6. & 7th days our sonus Killed their swine samuell was at poquatuck I was at the farme the .8. day the Rams wer: brought from the Island its beeing fryday: the .9th day Augustine was heare with his boat and steeven Wilcoks my Wife went in the boate to new London sam fecthed Whome the Canoow: the .10th. day was the greate Tyde the .11th. day monday I fecthed my Wife from new London the .14 day I brought beans from the farme the .15. day friday I fecthed .3 loads of wood: the .20. day samuell brought whome the swine: 21. I was at new London: 22. friday wee fecthed the seder boults: .23. wee drawed Timber for the meeting house sabath day .24. mr noyce Taught first after he came from the bay Tusday .26. Hanah was verie ile in her face samuell went to fflemings: Thursday the 28. day we killed our Swine ffrancis Thorne was ap(re)hended friday .29. saterday the .30. day my Canoow was at mr Chesters vesel.

The tenth moneth is december and hath .31. days sabath day the first: the .6. day I was att new London sabath day the .8. monday the 9 and the .10th I was at new London Leeftenant samuell mason sent Two swine sabath day the .15. sacrament day the .16. day we brought Clement and William minor to Tagwoncke The .17. day Clement went whome & had A Cow with him the .18. day I begun to Thresh wheate the 28 day I winowed & had 17. bushells of winter Wheate the 26 day we had a Court at mr stantons the 30. day monday I was at mill with 2 bushells of wheat and 2. of Indean corne my Wife went to new London Tusday the 31 The .17 day Lam had the steere.

The leventh moneth is Januarie and hath .31. days wensday the first: and wensday the .8. I made an End of threshing of winter wheate and Rie thursday .9th Clement was heare saterday the .11th. he went whome hee had the Two mares and the Coult with him monday the .13th. wee Cleared the Trees about the new meeting house and wensday the .15. & the .16. days wee Raysed the meetting house Tusday .21. wee winowed oats .38. bushells & an halfe Robert ffleming mended the sadle wensday .22. thursday 23. wee had a Court at samuell Cheesbroughs the 24th was the great storme of rayne: 29. wensday friday the .31. I had fouer score bushells of oats & three

The twelfe moneth is februarie and hath .28. days saterday the first: the 4th day Tusday I was at new London I had Two paier of playne shews of mr Royce I owe him Two shillings saterday the .8. samuell was at the farme Thursday the .13th wee wer at the new meeting house and appoynted how many seats to make friday the 14 wee agreed with goodman wheeler for £26. to make the seats to Cart and pvide all about them but nayls: saterday the .15. I fecthed all the Iron workes from Lam there was due to him 02-06-00: and the steere payd for wensday the .19. I looked out and picthed upon a place for my fiftie ackers Thursday the 20th Clement and martha was maried by mr withrell Comr saterday 22 and friday the 28.

The first moneth is march and hath .31. days sater-day the first and is the second yeare after the Leap yeare and is ye yeare of our Lord .1673. and from the Creation .5622. and the .25. yeare of the Reigne of

our Lord King Charles the second munday the 3d. I
would have had my .50. ackers Layd out and could
not: the .2 day mr noyce first taught at the new meeting house the .8. day saterday samuell sould his Skins
goodman searles fecthed hay I threshed pease it
snowed: saterday the .15. the Carpenters pay was put
aboard mr Chester I Ended my Threshing & burned
the hill on the Corne field and friday the .21. I tooke
up mr buls pibald hors our Children was all heare
from Tagwounck my wives arme was burnt and saterday the .22. 23 the sacrament at new London Tusday
.25. my wife was taken verie sike goodwife searles
watched with her the .29. saterday I fecthed Corne
from the wapasqua monday .31. it snowed samuell
was at London Lohan and denis fecthed .12. hundred
of hay

The second moneth is Aprile and hath .30. days
Tusday the first: hanah ould Kow saterday the 5.
wee brought the mares whome to marke the bay
mares Coult: samuel Holmes fecthed mr Bulls pibald
Horse the .8. day Tusday I was at the farme and Let
the medow and corne field to Joseph morgaine for
.30. bushels of corne and to keep me: 24. Catle this
somer I Joseph and samuel Renewed all our Corner
Trees the same day Clement and his wife was heare
the .15. day Tusday I sowed the white pease The

white (faced) mare foled samuell grafted trees at his orchard the .17. Thursday I sowed oats at the beech & diged up the hops friday the .18 I made an End of sowing oats & the Indean sayd samuell mason sa(i)d sumething about pupsonup and Tusday .22. we looked the white heighfer wensday .23. I was 65. years ould wensday the .30. wee did driv mr Richardsons neck I turned out the bay mare.

may is the third moneth and hath .31. days Thursday the first: Thomas park Tould me that Joseph morgaine would leave the farme Thursday the Eight day I made yard door the Squas weeded at the little orchard and saterday the 10 I was at new London for firkins monday 12 I was to mill: Thursday the .15. the Coult died friday the .16. samuell was at the farme there fell haile Twice that day and it did Thunder and Lighten I was puting boughs upon the stone wale Thursday .22. wee met at mr Richardsons about Baldwins business wensday .28. a fast through out the Colony Thursday .29. I tooke Com'r's oath: wee shore the sheepe saterday the .31.

Thursday the .19. of June Robert Burrows was maried and Joseph stanton.

June is the fouerth moneth and hath .30. days sabath day the first monday I went to new London and Taried there all the week sabath day mr hayns and mr fflecher Taught at our meeting house it being the Eight day mr Knight was heare: and sabath day the .15. and sabath day the .22. there was a sacrament att new London the same weeke wee begun to mow sabath day .29. monday the .30. wee began to make hay the same day goodm(an) burrows was maried the .19th. of June and Joseph stanton as it is sayd.

The .18 day of July being friday Hanah mended the hearth mr samuell Cheesbrough was buried the .31. day of July .1673

July the fift moneth and hath .31. days Tusday the first wee made hay in the bottome Abrame had the last of his fouer pounds the .5. day the ould woman was Cared whome samuell was at the farme it being saterday Lidea was heare: Tusday the .8. mr Brodstreet taught at Arons wensday the .9. Clement had away his Children Tusday .15. mr stanton fecthed mee to mr Baldwin Tho park was heare wee had nine Loads of hay in the barne friday the .18. my wife was at new London Tusday .22. wee had Reaped Ry and it Reigned verie much the 23. I was with samuell Cheesbrough Tusday .29. wee made an End Reaping all but the sumer wheate Deckon parks and his Two brothers was heare Thursday the .31.

Agust the sixt moneth and hath .31. days friday the first saterday the second I had .1000. wheate

sheafes and .460. Rie sheafes into the barne and
made an End of harvest the 8 day I was at new
London it being friday: the .14. day I made goodman
Lam his will we had harrowed the Rie ground wee
had A Letter from John williams was com with
powder fryday the .15. Thursday the .21. Josephs
second daughter was borne friday .22. sam sowed
wheate Tho park bought the swine at the farme friday .29. I harrowed the wheate ground & ould mrs
Cheesbrough departed this world sabath day the .31.
the sacrament is to be Administred at new London

The seventh moneth is september and hath .30.
days the first is monday the 2 day mr Brodstreet did
Teach at Arons: and pmiseth to teach there the first
Tusday in october: sunday the 7th mr Richardson
taught at our meeting house & monday the .8. day
we had .3. mowers and Ended mowing monday the
.15. I sowed Rie and mr noyce was to goe to the bay
I was to goe unto new London the .19. day I came
from the Court monday .22. and Tusday .23. wee
were about Carry busines wensday .24. I was at
Crandalls mill 25 Thursday I made a barle of sider
monday the .29. our sonns went to the Bay I was at
mashuntucks Tusday the 30: :

October is the Eight moneth and hath .31. days
wensday The first and wensday the .8. I was at hart-

ford wensday the .15. I was at moshuntucks wensday .22. wee wer carring of muck the 24 friday I fecthed Turneps we brought whome the whit faced heighfer friday the .31. I brought the white heighfer from Cheesbroughs.

The ninth moneth is november hath .30. days the first is saterday: wensday the .5. was A day of Thanksgiveing: Thursday the .6th. day the Indeans wer heare about Renolds Kow and fffeminss Corne saterday the .8. wee fecthed pales: wensday the .12. I was at new London the .14. day wee made an End fecthing of pales Daniell mason mare broke her Legg saterday the .22. wee made an End plowing the Rie stuble in the playne the 26. 27. 28 wee plowed in the playne: 29. saterday the 2 snow fell sabath day the 30: :

The Tenth moneth is december and hath .31. days the first is monday I was att mill the 4 day wee put up the swine monday the .8. day we be to Run the 2 miles from the ould meeting house: and Thursday the .11. A day of humilliation and monday the .15. we plowed in the playne monday 22 we Layd out six hundred Ackers of Land for Elihu Cheesbrough: we killed our swine The same day 23 day the Comitee met at Renolds monday .29 hanah was at new London wensday .31. Clement and manaseth came to us: :

Januarie is the Leventh moneth and hath .31. days
Thursday the first saterday the third Clement and
manaseth went whome I delivered the wal eide mare
and the blacke Eared Cow to manaseth: the .9th
day friday Ephraim saw Manases wal eide mare the
mustering was beare—I pilated in Mr Brewster

Thursday the .15. the .16. day the Catle came from
the Creeke Thursday the .22. I had Threshed Two
Ackers of winter wheate wee had In all .38. bushells
Thursday .29. saterday .31 we had one Lam: the .6th
of februarie it was Reported that marie Tong had a
young Sonn.

The Twelvth moneth is ffebruarie and hath .28.
days sabath day the first monday the 2d I begun to
thresh Rie the .6. day friday I made an End of
threshing of Rie sabath day the .8. thursday the .12.
day I made an end of threshing the Loose oats: my
wifes shewes wer brought: saterday the .14. we had
Leters Came post to pres souldiers and sabath day
the .15. monday they marcht of and Thursday .19.
and the .20. I diged stones sam Rode to Mistick:
sabath the 22. Tusday .24. I made an End of Threshing of oats

march is the first moneth and hath .31. days sabath
day the first and is the third after the Leape yeare:

and the yeare of our Lord 1674: and from the Creation 5623. and sabath day the .8. the .9th. monday
we mended the Cart bridge Tusday the 10th. we had
a Court at Nehemiah palmers saterday the .14. we
wer examining Roger sterie sabath day the .15. the
.16. day we Examined ffleming the .18. wensday we
kept it a day of humilliation at moses palmers the
.19. day Thursday Tho Bell and I set all Even sabath
day .22. I sowed oats the .23. monday Tusday 24. a
Court at Nehemiahs house sabath day the .29 Litle
Ephraim had scalded himselfe Tusday the 31. manaseth went whome we wer plowing for Oats we had
Lost Two yearlings: :

The second moneth is April and hath 30. days
wensday the first the 6th I carried stones the .7th.
tusday I was at mill the 8th day wensday osbornes
weding was and the 15. day wensday I toke bond for
marie osbornes appearance: the .20. day wee Read
the Letter at samuell parks the .21. I was at mill:
wensday .22. mr Noyse was heare wensday the 29. I
Rune the bounds with Isack wheeller and on Thursday the 30. my wife went to Tagwonk Ephraims
daughter was borne

The third moneth is may and hath .31. days friday
the first this weeke I made my Cart fryday the .8. a
Towne meeting monday the .11. I and my wife was

at New London friday the .15. we pulled ˙down the Chimblies monday the .18. day Thomas park begun to build friday .22. wee shore the sheep and had whome one of the mantle Trees friday .22. 25 we had A Towne meeting: 27. wensday we Layd out bay grants on the Est side poquatuck friday .29. saterday 30 sabath day 31:

The .15. day of Agust Joseph brought his swine

The fouerth moneth is June hath .30. days monday the first we wer warned To a Towne meeting this weeke The Court at New London I carried Two bushells of wheat The .8. day monday and monday the 15 my wife went to new London the .16. John Renolds had atachment and monday the 22 day wee mad an End of the Chimney and 23d wee finished the Entrie Joseph helped us monday 29 I caried a firkin of buter to Joshua Raymond it weighed 66. pound I had my horse shewed and the .29. and Abram began to mow Tusday the 30:

the .15. of July .1674. I payd to Tho: Wheeler one pound 14s by benit and 6s by Tho Edwards

The fift month is July hath .31. days the first is wensday friday the third samuell went to Coneticut the 5 day the sacrament was at New London the .8th day wensday friday the .10. day samuell Came whome

the same day wee had .7. Loads of Hay in the barne
my wife was Ile in her heade and monday the .13. I
and my wife was at New London wensday the .15. a
Court at Mistick wee Reaped Rie that day wensday
the 22. the 23d it Rained we Ended the summer
wheate the 29 being wensday my wif was at New
London friday the 31

The sixt moneth is Agust hath .31. days saterday the first: the sixt day wee had a Towne meeting
the books wer delivered to goodman fish the .7. day
I was at New London saterday the .8. mr John
stanton and Leeftenet mason feethed the greate
bookes it being the 15 day and saterday Ephraim was
heare Monday the 17. wee feethed hay our staple
broke friday wee the Com r s had been three days
about signing of bills and saterday the .22. Tho bell
had been 3 days makeing my wasket Samuel was in
the bay James had two sows the .25 samuell came
whome the .27. day I was at pequant saterday .29. I
was ill sabath day the 30 monday .31.

The yeare .74. I had .50 bushells of wheate

The seventh moneth is september and hath .30.
days the first is Tusday Tusday the .8. the messengers came wensday the .9th. much agetation Thursday the .10th. the ordination was to be: and monday

the .14. I sowed wheate Tusday the .15. I went to Court Tusday .22. I came from the Court John his wife and Children came hither: 26 I gathered the peares winowed the seed Rye it being satterday

The 20th of october .1674. the mares were put aboard the Ketch for Coneticut.

The Eight moneth is October and hath .31. days the first is Thursday: John and his wife and Children were still heare this weeke we gathered our Apels hanah went to New London our sons Lost theyr Catle Thursday the .8. there was an hard frost monday the 12 day John went away Thursday the 15 I was presing Cider saterday .17. I made an End mr Adams vesell was to take in the water and Hay the .18. day was the second sabath mr noyse was wanting and Thursday the .22. sabath day 25. I was att New London: Thursday the 29. the .28. day of Thanksgiveing I was at New London saterday the 31. I was at Lams with Corne

The ninth moneth is November and hath .30. days sabath day the first: and sabath day the .8. mr Noyse Taught out of the .14th. of mark the .18. the sabath before I was at New London: and sabath day the 15. 9. Children baptised wensday the .18. a day of Thanksgiveing the 20th of November all Accounts ballanced at Lathams and payd sabath day the 22. Thursday .26. I had 2000 of Nayls at mr Raymonds: The .30 of this month Clement and manaseth were heare

The .9th of December was a day of humilliation upon the Contrie List .196. 10. 00. 1674

The Tenth month is December and hath .31. days Tusday the first: Tusday the 8 day wee had a Court and monday the 14. we killed the swine and the 15 day Tusday wee had a Court the great snow fell: and the 21 day a court at the widows: Tusday .22. I was threshing sumer wheate: the .29. day Tusday a towne meeting To Chuse Towne officers: Thursday .31. wensday the .30. day of December 1674 I payd five bushells of wheat to mr Noyse for the yeare one Thousand seventie five

The 30. of December 1674 A meeting at Nathaniell Cheesbroughs

Januarie the Leventh moneth and hath .31. days friday the first: and friday the .8. day wee had .30. bushells of wheate of sumer wheate there was a Court at the widows and friday the .15. wee winowed winter wheate .23. bushells: payd to ffrinke .3£ in Indean Corne and Rie ate 3 s 6 d p bushell Indean Corne 3 s p bushell ffriday .22. wee had .14. bushells

of Rie monday 25. wee went to ffrinks the 27. the
meeting was ate our house it being wensday: ffriday
29 sabath day .31. samuell was at New London

The first of ffebruarie .1674. I begune the yeare
with Carie Latham: :
†††††††††††††††††††-------

februarie the Twelfth moneth and hath .28. days
monday the first: monday the 8 I was at New London
the .9th day I winowed oats and had .35. bushels
Thursday the .11. day the Church met at Ephraims:
the .12. day friday Joseph and his Tenn bushells of
Corne sabath day the 14 day it is shrove sunday and
volantins day: The sacrament of baptisme was administred to Nehemiah palmer and young Tho: stantons
Children the 17 day is to be a meeting at the widow
Cheesbroughs being wensday the .18. day I was at
wheelers the 21. day the sacrament of the Lords super
the 2 d Time monday 22. the 28. day was sabath day
Ephraims wife was ppounded to the Church: The .8.
day it snowed an(d) ould wheeler came to Reckon
with gershum: the 15 day of march ould wheeler owed
to goodwife ffaning and his daughter in Law that he
p'mised pay the next Rate

The first moneth is march and hath .31. days monday the first: and is the yeare .1675. and Leap yeare:
and from the Creation .5624. the first day I burned

about the house ate the farme the .4th. day Thursday
I caried .5. bushells of Corne to John Serles The .8.
day is monday I was goeing to New London for wheels
the .12th day ffriday I payd 10 bushells of wheat to
mr Raymond: munday the 15 samuell was at pine
Island Tusday the .16. I was at mill the .17. day it
Rayned mr Richardson was heare the 18 day Thursday I payd mr stanton .10 shillings in wheate The .22.
day monday samueles .30. acker Lott was Layd out
wensday .24. our wheels wer brought & Thursday .25.
we had mark the white faced mares Coult a hors Colt
white face four white ffeet one black hoofe part of the
Tayle white: the 28. day the sacrament was adminestred monday 29. wensday 31 the meeting was heare

The second moneth is Aprile and hath .30. days
Thursday the first: Daniell Crum and sarah Harrish
wer maried Tusday the 6th I was att New London and
A Towne meeting the same day the order about the
Rate for one peny on the pound was Interpreted
Thursday the .8th mr Linde was heare monday the
.12th wee brought whome samuels horse the 14. day
Hanahs Cow died Thursday the .15. it was wet: and
monday the .19. wee wer at New London Tusday the
20th I sowed oats and pease in the playne and Thursday the .22. I sowed wheate: friday the .23. day I was
.67. yeares ould I made an End of sowing I and my

wife went to see Rebecka Ephraims daughter: wee
wer on wensday Laying out mr payns Thursday .29.
wee wer Laying out Lands friday the .30

The third moneth is may and hath .31. days saterday the first: we Layd out omeganset meadow monday
the third day mr griswold went whome there was 30s
due for my 5 days worke saterday the .8. day wee
made an End in the orchard monday the 10th. my
wife and I was at fannings manaseth was heare for
his mare: ffriday the 14. wee Looked Hanahs mare
and was at manasses meadow and found Lams horse
Hanah was at the ffarme and saterday the .15. mr
Richardson would have an Atachment upon mr Noyses
his Land Tusday the 18 day samuell went to help
Ephraim friday the 21 we had our Calfes to Tagwonck saterday the .22. wee wer weeding in the
playne the 27 day we Layd out Land for deackon
park the .28. for Captaine prentice: saterday the .29.
monday .31

The fouerth moneth is June and hath .30. days:
Tusday the first wensday the .2d a day of humiliation Thursday the .4 I was at the Court saterday the
.6. I came whome Tusday the .8. I was at mill wensday the .9. I was at mr noyse his house saterday 12.
samuell came whome I and my wife was at Tagwonke:: Tusday the .15. goodman ffrink begun the

porch: 16. day I was at Arons the widow Cheesbrough was maried I brought whome the cheesfat:
mr Noyse was brought abed the .20. day it was
sabath day: Tusday the .22. day we Raysed the
porch: monday .(2)8. Tusday .29. the leters came
from mr Williams to the govenor and Council I and
benjamin was at New London wensday the 30. the
garison was broken up: the .3. of July sabath day the
.4th of July Leeftenant omsteed came to my house
with the Draggoonors

The fift moneth is July and hath .31. days: Thursday the first—Tusday the .6. day the major was
heare with his Troop and Thursday ye 8 day The
Troop is to set fforth Thursday the .15 wee came
whome I was .8. days out myselfe and Two Horses
wensday .21. a day of humilyation Thursday .22.
wee made .8. great Cocks of Hay Thursday the .29.
wee begun to Reape Rie wee had seven Loads of
Abrams hay whome saterday 31::

The 17 day of Agust it was agreed that I should
Take 80 l of Leade to mr Richardson accordingly
the .20. day friday I Tooke it::

The sixt moneth is Agust and hath .31. days
sabath day the first Thursday the .5. day Abram and
James went after philip saterday the .7th. we had
Cut our oats wee had .670. sheaves .300. Rie sheaves

and sabath day the .8. day wensday the 11th. wee had .420 sheaves of sumer wheat and sabath day the .15. the Debate was about the Draggoonors Tusday the 17 a towne meeting the 18 day wee wer at New London sabath day the .22. The .27. we Raysed the Cider press the 28. it was wet sabath day .29. T(h)e greate storme of winde and high Tide pierces vessell Cast away at poquatuch beech much Lost of Corne and Hay. multitudes of Trees blowen downe Tusday 31:

The seventh moneth is september and hath .30. days wensday the first: the .7. day the lists were to be brought in the pequit Indeans set forth for Coneticut wensday the .8. day the .9th. day is to be kept a day of humiliation by the church: the .15. day is to be kept a day of humiliation for this country of every month till the Court see cause to alter it wensday the 15. leeftenat mason sent horses to squmatuck the 18. day saterday I was at New London and Carried Two firkins of buter to mr Raymond the 20. monday a towne meeting should be wensday .22. we made the Reeck on the fur side the Hill: sabath day .26. the Lords supper was administred leeftenant averie was heare thursday the 30:

The .7th. of october 1675 the Constable had A way my white hors upon a press account

The Eight moneth is october and hath .31. days ffriday the first: the .6. we met to Chuse deputies and I was at the Examination of Ezekiel mayne: the .8. day is ffryday: wee put in Ten young Catle in to mr Richardsons field on the .15. day being friday: the 22. day I was at New London I had .15. pound of sugar of mr Raymond I Receved 5 letters from bristoll wee wer fortifiing our house friday 29. wee had a Towne meeting and had the Election Court orders Reade satterday the .30. I was at meshuntapit The .29. day the generale Court orders was published: an(d) friday the fift of november Leeftenant mason wente to the bay and Henry steevens: the Constabls warant was Torne the .6d. mr Richardson and the Constable fell out

The ninth moneth is November and hath .30. days: monday the first the third day I was ordayned Leeftenant of the dragoonors: and under pay for that service the Com'r's met at New London monday the .8th. Tusday the .9. the souldiers were apoynted to meet heare about 10. or .12. oClock: the 10 day wee wer at Captayne Averies the 13 day saterday John Averie was heare it was wet: the 12. day of this moneth the Rames were brought from the Island monday the .15. fryday the 19th I sent to Captayne Averie the News the 17th was a day of humiliation:

monday .22. wee Killed Two Cows: the .21. Captayne pembleton sayd that suckqunce would not deliver the captives: monday .29. wee Looked Catle found fouer or five John Averie was married the .30. day Tusday I was at meshuntup wee killed the swine

The Tenth moneth is December and hath .31. days wensday the first : : wensday the 8. it was a day of humilliation The 9. day Ephraims 3d sonn was borne all The souldiers were to be billited at the Contries Charge horse and man wensday the .15. Coneticut Armie Set forth from mr Richardsons

from the .8. of december to the .8. of ffebruarie I was Imployd in the Contries service about the Indean warr besides 8 days in the sumer hors and man and my white hors Ten days being prest for John gallop.

The eleventh moneth is Januarie and hath .31. days saterday the first: : The .21. the major went to Norwich I was at New London and samuell saterday 22. monday 24. mr Richardson Cut out my Coat The Rest of this moneth I spent in the war

The .17. of ffebruarie .1675. the souldiers were apoynted to goe forth

The 2d of march 1675. 76 the papers Concerning Takeing the Townes bills for the Charge of warr came first to my hand

The Twelvth moneth is ffebruarie and hath 29. days: it being Leap yeare Tusday the first monday the .7th. I came whome from the war and Tusday the 8 Tusday the 15. wee came from the meeting at New London about the souldiers goeing out wensday the .16. the Constable Tould me yt hee was to provide .12. souldiers of this Towne for Captayne Denison Tusday the .22. the .23. is apoynted to (be) a day of humiliation Tusday .29. I was at New London they were makeing up theyr accounts with the Contrie for the souldiers The 28 day I sowed sumer wheate

The first moneth is march and hath .31. days wensday the first and it is the first yeare after the Leap yeare and the yeare of our Lord .1676. and from the Creation .5625 the first day the prisoners were delivered to major palmes the 2. day wee chose Townesmen the 3 day I was at mill the 7th day Tusday the volenteers were to meet at meshuntupit and the .13. day of march they Returned wensday the .15. I harrowed in the wheate in the playne wensday the 22 was a day of humilliation through the whole Collony the garison souldiers came heare Thursday the 23. saterday the 25 and our Ladie day monday 27 wee wer to be at New London .28. wee wen to Norwich wensday 29. Thursday 30 friday 31::

The 28. of march Tusday wee set forth and cam

whome the .4. of aprile Tusday wensday I went to Coneticut and came whome saterday

The second moneth is April and hath .30. days satterday is the first and saterday the .8. monday the .10 and saterday the .15. wee were preparing for another Jorney to the Indeans at Narraganset the 17 day to meet at Meshuntupit beeing monday and saterday .22. wee wer at Cooeeset the 27. Thursday wee were free and Ended our business at New London saterday 29. samuell was at New London sabath day the 30: :

The 23d of Aprile .1676. Tho minor was .68. yeares ould

The third moneth is may hath .31 days monday the first: the .2d. 3d. and fouerth days I was at New London and brought amonition and bread for the Expedition to the Indeans: monday the Eight day Tusday the .9th. wee went to meshuntuck monday the .15. wee came from providence the .16. day Now London souldiers went whome Thursday the .18. I payd mr noyse .4. bushells of wheate and .3. bushells of Rie in -1-12-00 fo(r) his Rate: and monday the 22. we fetched the Catle into the pastor wensday 24. a day of humiliation Thursday .25. wee washed sheep monday .29. wee sheered our sheep Tusday .30 samuell and hanah was at New London wensday .31.

The fouerth moneth is June and hath .30. days the
first is Thursday.   I was at New London samuell
went to Norwich Thursday the .8. wee Turned out
the oxen Thursday the .15. wee were to meet all the
souldiers at steeven Richardsons house sabath day
the .18. the souldiers came whome to Stoneingtone
the .21. day we mowed the Litle orchard Thursday
the .22. saterday .24. midsumer day: samuell came
whome from the Armie Tusday .27. samuell went
forth Interpreter to the Armie the second time wensday .28. a day of humilliation Thursday .29. friday
.30. Captayne Averie and his wife was heare

The fift moneth is July and hath .31. days saterday is the first wensday the .5. day samuell came
whome from the Armie sick the 8 day was saterday
Captayne Denison was heare it was wet saterday the
.15. wee brought whome wood the .22. saterday I
ffetched whome the prisnors from the queens Towne
our sonn John was heare the 23d day the Armie
marched of from mashantuckset the .26. day wee
had all our wheat in .740. sheaves: : saterday the .29.
our sister Sloan came wee wer at plowin in the
playne monday the 31 wee went to quaquatage: :

The .17. of Agust .1676. wee Caried Away the .3.
Rams: The .18. day Tho: sha was buried mr birchid
was heare: :

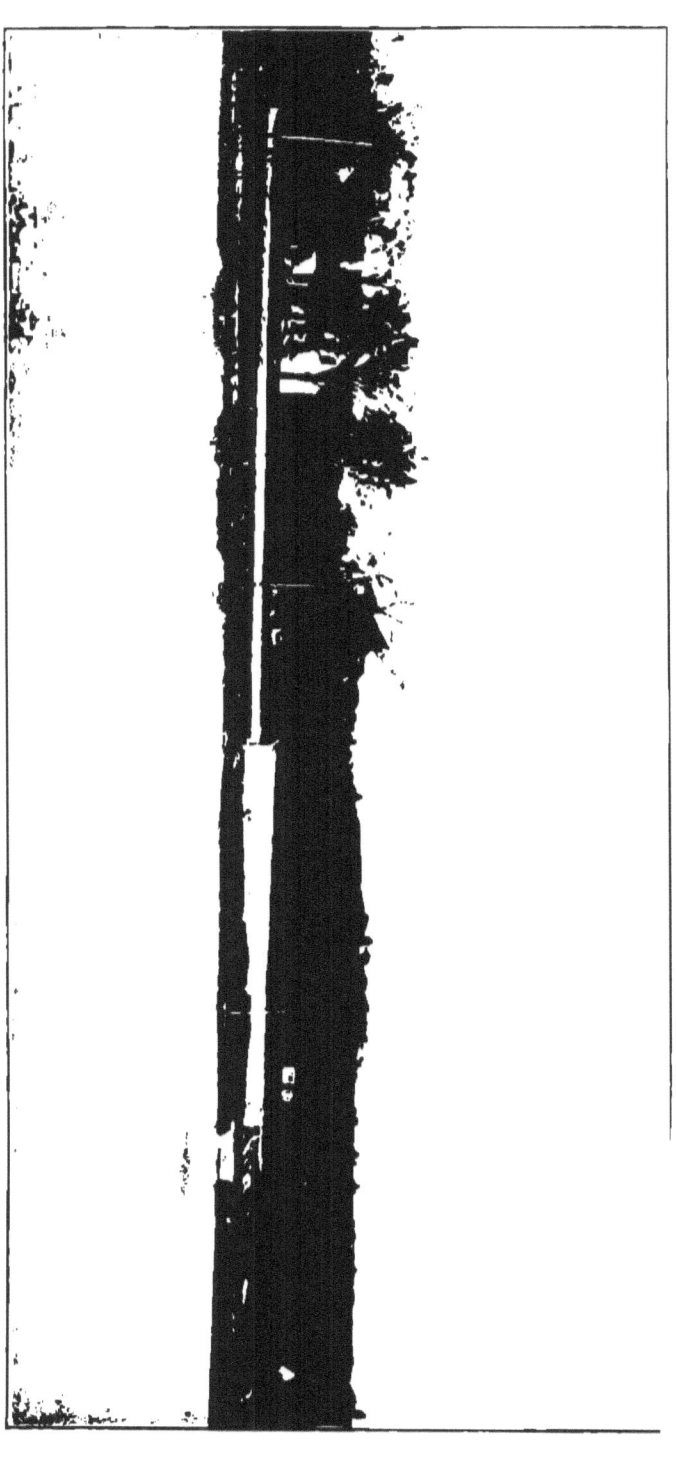

Site of Thomas Minor's House on Quiambaug Cove.   The third house on same site is now occupied by Cornelius Miner.

The sixt moneth is Agust and hath .31. days the first is Tusday the first the 2 day was a fast the .4th day I was at mill the .7. day wee put forth our Calves Tusday the .8. I hurt my back sister Averie was heare the .9. day wensday stoneington souldiers came whome wee had .6. sheepe killed with the wolfe monday the .14. Thomas ffaning was heare to mow: Tusday the .15. I was at mill wensday the .16. it was apoynted to be a publick day of Thanksgiveing over the whole Colony Tusday .22. wensday 23. a day of Thanksgiveing .29. wensday .30. a day of Thanksgiven in the Colony Thursday .31.

The seventh moneth is september friday is the first and hath .30. days: friday the .8. day I carted Hay the .10. day was the Lords super adminintred friday the .15. I caried poles gershum Palmer was heare friday .22. I was at the County Court wensday .27. a day of publick thanksgiveing: saterday the .30.

for ffering with Carie Latham from the .5. of december .1676.   †††††††††††††††††------

Tusday the .19. of december .1676 I payd mr Hide six shillings six pence for Two paier of specttecles no cases

The Eight moneth is october and hath .31. days sabath day the first sabath day the .8. wee was at

yeomans about the Cow: monday the .9. I tooke up
the pay for the .2. oxen sabath day the .15. monday
.16. I was at New London sould my oats wensday
.18. I sould my bull stag sabath day .22. the .2 mar-
chants was at mr Richardsons monday .23. we begun
to Carie muck sabath day .29. monday .30. deliverance blackman had Johns Letter The same day I
received one Ancker of mallaces .6 Pound of sugar
.2 quarts of Rum: of perker delivered to his sonn
Jonathan .27. bushels of oats and ½ still due to mee
from mr perker one barle of mallaces and all is Even
Tusday the .31. the .30th of this moneth our Rams
were brought whome

The Ninth moneth is November and hath .30. days
wensday the first it was a day of Thanksgiven Thursday the .2d wee wer about gallops Land and manaseth came heare monday & the 6 day wee met billings
with samuells steere as hee was goeing to the bay and
wensday the 8 the 7th day Daniel Crum and Rachell
Roberts were maried wensday the .15. was a day of
humilliation Thursday the .16. a greate storme sabath
day the .19. wee had A sacrament the 21 day I
was at New London wensday 22. Thursday .23. manaseth went whome monday the .27. Aron start Junior
and mehitable shaw were maried .28. a towne meet-

ing to publisk Court orders wensday .29. Thursday 30 there was a snow fell

The tenth moneth is december and hath .31. days the first is friday. This weeck wee killed our steere and swine I was ill in my back friday the .8. day and friday the .15. the Committee met at Norwich monday the 18. wee drove our Catle to Tagwounck wensday the .20th we met at mr Noyse his house and agreed to pay for the wine. 1 s a man. 11 of us for the yeare Ensueing friday the 22 Captayne Chapman was heare: Captayne dennison came whome I begun to Thresh sumer wheat 23. day our dogg was shot Thursday .28. a meeting to Chuse Constables the same day I payd mr Noyse .7. bushels of wheate .35. Towards his Next yeares Rate. sabath day the .31.

The leventh moneth is Januarie and hath .31. days monday the first sabath day the .7th. the order from the Councell was published munday the .8th. wee Caried up Joseph his Corne friday the .12th. manaseth was heare with the guns munday the .15. and wensday the .17. our first Lectuer was at the meeting house Thursday the .18. day I made an end of threshing wheate we had .36. bushels ½ sabath day .21. the Lords super was administred but .12. Comunicants appeared. monday .22. 23. we visited our Neighbors: moses was sicke: monday 29 30. day wee wer at mr Noyses sister Averie was heare: wensday .31. I winnowed oats. the 15 of march 1676-77 hanah came from New London

The Twelfth moneth is ffebruarie and hath .28. days Thursday the first and is the first yeare after the Leape yeare wensday the .7th. lectuer day Thursday the .8. day monanup and his son Returned friday the 9 day I payd benjamin palmer for Hanah bodies Thursday the .15th. day I was at weequatequk and at babcots and The 18 and 19 Thomas Averie was heare: and Thursday the 22 friday the .23. we fecthed whome the horse monday the .26. a Towne meeting about a smith samuel sent his Corne to mr baldwin Thursday the .28. day Nathaniell park and sarah geares were maried it was our Lectuer day the 28 day wensday

The first moneth is march and hath 31. days Thursday the first: it is the secend yeare after the Leape yeare: from the Creation .5626. and the yeare of our Lord .1677. Tusday the .6. day I was at mr Sanders. Thursday the .8. day wee begun to plow in the playne Thursday .15. there was a Court warned but the select men came not only Nathaniell Cheesbrough the .16 & 17. days wee Cast mucke and burned ground Thursday .22. I had my plow Irons mended wee had sowed all our whete Thursday .29. 30 day I

was at mill .31. day saterday we plowed the wheat
stuble.

The second moneth is Aprill hath .30. days sabath
day the first: this weecke wee made an End of plowing in the playne sabath day the .8. wee had the sacrament of the Lords super: this day the Constables
prest men the 10. day I was at New London and
Thursday the .12. day our sister Sloan went away the
same day Captayne Denison marcht of the .14. he
came whome sabath day the .15. day and sabath day
the .22. the .23d I was 69. yeares ould: the 25 I was
at New London The 28. 29. mr willis was heare
sabath day the .29. monday the 30

The .19. day of Januarie 1679 80 I delivered to
Jonathan perker .30. bushells of oats to be payd in a
barle of good malases and other barbades goods.

Due to mr parker of New London this 2d day of
June 1677 to be payd in butter for .14. pound of
Coten woll and .3 quarts of Rum -01-05-00

The .21. of ffebruarie 1677-78 I Received of Mr
Lindes upon mr perkers account fouer pounds of
Coten woole five shillings

of mrs perker six pound of sugar -00-03-00 the 3d
of July .1678. I recevid one barles of malasses 20

pound of Cotten: 20 pound of sugar six pound of sugar: 2 quarts of Rum: 2 bushels of salt (canceled.)

The second day of June 1677 I delivered to mr parker at New London Twentie five bushels of oats. That is to say Twentie bushels for a barle of mallaces Two quarts of Rum and six pound of sugar To be payd at his coming whome: and The other five bushels to be payd in other pay after Two shillings six pence a bushell: only one quart of Rum is alredy payd Towards the five bushels The .17. day of July delivered one firkin of buter

The .21. of ffebruarie mr. Ralph perker had ffowertie one bushells of oats (canceled) weighed .76. pound that is 01-12-00 one quart of Rum samuell had -(canceled)

The Third moneth is may hath .31. days the first: Tusday the .8. wensday .9. I went to Hartford: Tusday the 15. and Tusday the .22. I came from Hartford goodman Searles and his wife was heare wee had a yew Lamed: The .27. day the sacrament of the Lords super was administred the .28. I was at New London there is due to mr perker 1-5-0 for Coten woole and Rum the same day I made Even with mrs Raymond Tusday .29. Thursday .31. a day of humilliation samuell went to bostowne. the court marshall is to meet at Leeftenant masons

The 2d of June .1677 I delivered to mr. perker at New London Twentie five bushells of oats Twentie bushels for a barell or Mallaces .2 quarts of Rum six pound of sugar to be payd at his coming whome. the other five bushels in other pay: one quart of Rum (blurred)

The fouerth moneth is June hath .30 days friday the first: the 2d day I was at New London friday the 8 saterday the 9th day I was at New London the .11th. day wee went to Naraganset and come whome the .15. da(y) to steeven Richardsons being friday monday the major and mr banks went to Norwich being the 18 day friday 22: wee met at mr Noyses I payd him 2 bushells of Indean Corne and one bushell of wheat that is all that was due: for this yeare friday .29. a meeting at mr Noyses saterday the .30. Rebeckah Averie was heare: mr Richardson was heare hee came from bostowne

The fift moneth is July hath .31. days sabath day the first: wee had the sacrament of the Lords supper administred saterday the 7. wee had hay into the barne sabath day the 8. saterday the .14. I had all the orchard hay into the barne my Hors was shewed sabath day the .15. the 16 day I was at mill The .21. wee broke our cart wee had Cut our oats and sabath day the .22. monday it was wet wensday 25 s. James day I cut my pease and the oats were all Cut: sabath day the .29. monday the 30 wee had all our wheate in .770. sheaves Tusday the .31: :

The .13. of Agust 1677 Joseph stanton and Hanah Lord was maried as steeven Richardson tould mee the .16. of december she was delivered.

The sixth moneth is Agust hath .31. days wensday the first: James willet was maried The .4. day wee had .8. Loads of Hay stackt up wensday the .8. day monday the .13. samuell and abram went to Tag-wonck to mow wensday the .15. saterday the .18. Captayne Avery was heare Tusday .21. wee caried away our Rams wensday .22. Thursday 30.. steeven Richardson and Hanah agreed about the gerle: friday .31. it was wet we had one barle of Cider pounded.

The seventh moneth is september hath .30. days saterday the first: wensday the .5. my hors was shewed the 2d time The .6. day we had a Towne meeting saterday the .8. the 9th day wee had the Lords super adminstred saterday the .15. monday the .17. saterday .22. monday .24. Thomas avery went to bostowne Thursday 27 A meeting to Chuse deputies and 28 I was at Thomas perks saterday .29. and mickelmas day sabath day the 30:

Tho: Averie and Hanah Minor was maried the. 22.

of october 1677: : 26 day I maried our sister Elizabeth sloan.

The .8th. moneth is october hath .31. days monday
the first and monday the .8 day wee went to mr mos.
and monday the 15. Thursday .18. Thomas Averie &
I was at the ffarme and at Thomas perks they Tould
mee that Thomas perks would have the mares and
friday the 19 I payd Two bushels ½ of Corne to
billings for Turneps and brought whome one bushell
of Turneps monday the .22. Ephraim and Hanah and
Josephs wife was heare the .27. I had 6. bushells of
Corne and one peck of Abrams. mr Noyse is gon
into the bay the 30th day William benit and Susana
bright was maried the .10th of october I put my
shoulder out of Joynt.

The Ninth moneth is November hath .30. days
Thursday the first: the .7. day my shoulder was set:
Thursday the .8. the .9. brother Avery and sister
were heare John Lam was buried monday the 12 I
was at mill: Thursday the .15. my Brother Jonah
palmer and his sonn samuell was heare and went
away. the .16. day goodwif bills was heare and
Thursday .22. monday .26. sam wente to the bay the
same day wee fetched the Rames whome Thursday
the .29. I lent steeven Richardson .24 £. of lead:

friday the .30. Tusday the 4th of December 1677 the storme of snow.

'. The .12. of ffebruarie 1677 I made Even with Carie Latham:

The Tenth moneth is december hath .31. days saterday the first: sabath day the .2d. mr Tho: stanton departed saterday the .8 day samuell came whome Tusday the .12. mr Noyse begun his Lectuer saterday the .15. The 19 day mr Noyse was heare saterday the .22. it was wet I wrot to my Cousin william minor and saterday .29. monday .31. Crary and Cristabele Gallop was maried

The .7th. of Januarie billings and ffish was heare Tho: stanton and John Denison tooke the grand Jurie oath

The leyenth moneth is Januarie hath 31. days Tusday the first the .2d was the Lectuer day Clement and manaseth was heare and Tusday the .8. day I had payd for mr Noyse .2. bushels of Corne to the smith .2. bushells to goodman searles the .10. day wee paid our mony for the wine the .13. day wee had the sacrament The .14. day I begun to thresh Tusday the .15. and Tusday the .22. sam was gon to Cheesbroughs .23. the Lectuer wee had whome the sleed Tusday

.29. Jonathan gilbert Tooke the prisers oath: Thursday 31 I made an end of threshing wheate

†††††††††---------------------sacrament

ffebruarie the Twelvth moneth hath .28. days: friday
the first the second yeare after the Leape yeare:
friday the .8. Tusday the 12. I was at New London
the .13. day our Lecter and a Court friday the .15.
gershum Cotrel and berthia wilcox. were maried the
.16. day I caried .2. bushells of corne and one bushell
of wheate to mr Noyse our Nayls were brought whome
friday 22. the 25 day I made an End of threshing
Tusday .26. denis Called had .12. pound and halfe of
woole to spin the .27. day wee met at mr Noyes
Thursday the .28. I made an End of Cleaving of
Capboard Joseph brought whome the gray mare

The first moneth is march hath .31. days friday the
first and the yeare of our Lord .1678. the third yeare
after the Leape yeare and from the Creation 5627.
The .2d. sacrament was administred the third day:
the .6. day the lectuer the .7. day the Towne meeting the .8. day fryday I sould my horse Two mares
friday the 15 the prisonor was aprhended the .20.
day I sowed wheate and oats in the playne friday the
.22. the .23. Thomas Averys house was raysed friday
the .29. sabath day the .31. prayd for Daniel stanton

The .5. of April I begun the yeare with Carie Latham for ffering.††††††††††------------------

The second moneth is April hath .30. days monday the first monday the .8. I caried one bushel of Corne and an halfe to Renolds for Hanah's box the .7. day the .3d. sacrament was administred and munday the .15. the Comitee measured gallops Land tusday .16. I was Taken Lame the .18 day Thursday a day of Humilliation monday the .22. wee tooke up Hanahs mare .23. I was seventy yeares ould the .24. day it snowed The .29. I was at New London Tusday .30. apoynted to Chuse Deputies

The .13. of Januarie 1679 I had payd to mr Noyse .8. bushels 80 of wheate and .3. bushels of pease .2-1-00 for his Rate in the yeare .1680

may is the Third moneth hath .31. days wensday the first: and wensday the .8. manaseth was heare The .9th. day the meeting was at mr Noyses: sabath day the .12. wee had the fouerth sacrament the .13. day Daniell masons wife was buried wensday the .15. Joseph was about the porch chamber and wensday .22. wet wether wheellers horse came into the feild wensday 29. Joseph son Benjamin begun to mend Thursday 30 John Denison was heare friday 31. the 29 day wee washed our sheep the 31 day I begun to

hew gises for the seller the .3d of June wee sowed
pease.

June is the fouerth moneth hath .30. days saterday
the first: wee shore our sheep and saturday the .8.
wee planted Cabeg plants wee turned ou(t) 4 calves:
one pide steer calfe one black Kow calfe with a white
Tayle and one black steere calfe with a white Tayle
the .12. day manaseth ffecthed wool saterday the .15.
the Indean begun the Chimney Ephraims wife was
heare the .19. day a day of humilliation the .23. day
wee had the .5. sacrament satterday the .22. day
Tusday .25. Hanah went to her owne house 27. I was
at new London saterday 29. sabath day .30.

The .8. day of July Thomas Avery brought his
fouer Calves hither.

July is the fift moneth. hath .31. days monday the
first: and monday the .8. day Tho Averie and hanah
was heare: wee made an End Laying the hearth in
the Litle hous the 9. day and monday .15. the
.17. day wensday the Turneps in the Litle yard was
sowen I had bin at mill mr Richardson and star was
heare: monday .22. 23. Hanah was heare monday 29.
wensday .31. wee had made an end of Reapeing wee
had Six gags of oats & .200. sheaves of wheate

The .5th. day of Agust .1678. william pots and Rebeckah Avery was maried.

August is the sixth moneth hath .31. days Thursday the first the meeting at mr Noyses: the .4th. day Sonday the sixt sacrament was administred and the .7th. day Leeftenant samuell mason tooke the Comisionrs oath the .8. day Thursday wee stoned the new well mrs Richardson was heare. Tusday the .13. Edmund ffaning and margaret: billings was maried: Thursday the .15. and Thursday .22. wee gave in our lists: monday 26. wee caried away our Rams: wee had ended our Hay Thursday .29. samuel was at New London: hanah was heare my wife was sick the .30. day a meeting of the Commitee

september is the seventh moneth hath 30. days sabath day the first: sabath day the .8. our busines about ffornication Tusday the .17. County Court at New London the .19. day Debrah was dead sabath day 22 and sabath day .29. and mickelmas day monday the .30:

The .9th. of october .1678. I payd all and balanced the accounts with Henrie Eli(o)t Tho: Minor

The 13. of November .1678. al ballanced Eli(o)t was .9. s. in my debt.

The Eight moneth is october hath .31. days Tusday

the first: samuell delivered his Two Kows to Henrie Eli(o)t sabath day the sixt day wee had the .7th. sacrament: the 7 day monday wee were to chuse de-putys Tusday the .8. Tusday .15. monday .21. I fecthed Two thousand of Nayls of Henrie Eli(o)t Tusday .22. I was at mill 24 day wee went to Tagwonck it was wet The 25. day peeter Chock came heare. 28 day we wer at New London .29. Tusday the .30. wee ffetched whome the Rams .31. a day of Thanksgiveing.

November is the Ninth moneth hath .30. days friday the first: the .4th. day peeter Chock went to his wife the 3d. samuell was Taken Sick ffriday the. 8. friday the .15. sabath day the .17. the .8. sacrament was administred wensday the .20. our samuell was strangely taken the Same day Colver an(d) billings was heare the same day there was magets many seen in the Tray of milke alive Thursday. 21. a of day humiliation in all the three Collonys ffriday .22. Nathaniell Cheesbrough departed and ffriday 29. Thomas wheeler had away his Two sheep saterday the .30. Hanah is to goe whome

22 of december samuell came to the meeting house

December is the tenth moneth hath .31. days sabath day the first wensday the 4th. wee kiled our

Kow the .5 day I was at New London with the Taner
the .7th. day wee looked the young Catle sabath day
.8. and sabath day the 15. my wife and I went both
to the meeting house and Left samuell at whome
ffryday the 20th. Isack wheeler fetched away his .2.
steers saterday .21. I spake with mr Noyse at deanes
sabath day the 22. monday .23. samuell was let
blood Tusday 24. Hanah was heare sabath day .29.
Tusday .31.

The .25. or .26. of march .1679. margret ffaning
was delivered of a Childe

The .21. of this moneth Nathaniell Cheesbroughs
Daughter died with the distemper

January is the leventh moneth hath 31. days wensday the first a snow and wet I begun to thresh wheate
sabath day the 5 wee had the .9 sacrament wensday
the .8. I was at mr Noyses the greate snow about his
Indean women: and wensday the .15. and wensday
22. a day of humillyation for this County the .23.
wee were at ququatag wee winowed wheate wee had
.32. bushells and an halfe wee were to publish the
Indeans the 24. day orders. monday .27. wee had
payd mr Noyse .8. bushels of wheate 30 day I was at
mill the .31.'day wee branded the black horse Coult
and Josepths bay geldin

februarie is the Twelvth month hath 28. days
saterday the first: the .6. day Thursday the Church
met at mr Noyses house about mr Richardson and
Captayne denison saterday the .8. the .12 day wensday I made an End of threshing of oats saterday the
15. the .19 day of ffasting the .21. day wee made mr
Noyses Rate .61. pound and broched the barel of
Cider saterday the 22. the .20. day Clement & Hanah
went whom and Joseph had samuels young mare saterday the .8. I tooke up the black mare

it was in the .5. day of march 78-79 mrs bruster
was buried the 12. day ffather avery was buried:
Henrie Eli(o)t was here to be maried Curtice brought
the wine

The ffirst month is march hath .31. days saterday
the ffirst and the yeare of our Lord .1679. and Leape
yeare and from the Creation .5628. and saterday the
.8. Joseph had Two bushells of oats the .12. day I
sowed wheate and had sowed pasneps. the .14. day
wee apoynted to make the Country Rate saterday the
.15. monday .17. I wrot to England Tusday the .18.
John babcock fecthed the Kow the 19 day the fast
saterday 22 Tusday .25. our Lady day Ephraim had
two bushels of oats: the .26. day I made an end of
sowing of English corne Thursday 27. day the meeting at mr Noyses saterday 29. sabath day the sacra-

ment was administred monday 31. it snowed the
govenor was at mr Richardsons

The second moneth is April hath .30 dayes Tusday
the first Tusday the .8 mrs Richardson goodwife
deane was heare Tusday the 15. wensday met maijor
winthroup ate the mill the 17 day I delivered the
deed of my fif(t)ie ackers of Land to gershum Cotrell
there is still due to mee Twenty shillings of mony the
.20. day Hanah son was borne Tusday .22. I was at
New London .23. I was .71. years ould saterday the
.26. my wife and Ann went to Hanahs hous and
caried ye bed: it being saterday Tusday the 29. we
Chose deputys wensday the 30:

the .3. of may .1679. Leeftenant mason Took .5.
botls of rum from an Indean yt sayd shee Took it of
mrs Livin

The Third moneth is may hath .31. days Thursday
the ffirst we met at mr noyses we layd out Jane babcocks land sabath day the .4th. wee had the sacrament adminestred the .6. day Tusday mr Richardson
and I set forth for Coneticut Thursday the 8. Thursday the .15. saterday .17. I came whome monday the
.19. I payd my Rate and sams and there was nineteen
shillings and Ten pence halpeny still due to us: the
.20. day leeftenant mason toke the Com r s oath.

Thursday .22. Thursday .29. saterday .31. Tho Avery and his wife went whome

The fourth month is June and hath .30. days sabath day the ffirst sabath day the .8. monday 9 wee shore our sheep sabath day the .15. mr John Richardson Taught at our meeting house the Church had som talk Co(n)cerning the meeting of the minesters the .16. day my wife Rod to mr Mosses: sabath day .22. Thursdday 26. day the meeting is to bee at mr Noyses the .29. day the sacrament of the lords supper was administred the .30 day I was warned to apeare at Hartford about his majesties speacall service: the second day of July wee were to set forth being wensday

The ffift moneth is July and hath .31. days Tusday the ffirst the 2d wee went to Coneticut the .6. day wee came whom the .8. the meeting at mr Noyses being tusday the ninth day wee perfected the Rate: Tusday the .15. Testimonies taken wensday the .16. the mee(t)ing at Norige wee begun to Cary Hay Thursday the .22. Thomas Avery brought hither his Calves .23. wensday I was at mill: the 28. day I was at new London tusday the 29. Thursday 31

the meeting at mr Noyses the 14 of Agust the .17. a sacrament it being sabath day the sixt month is Agust and hath .31. days ffriday the first tusday .5. day wee all our oats in wensday the .6. day wee had all our wheate .800. sheaves Thom averie was heare ffriday the .9. day we had all our Calves in mond the .11. our Rams were Carried to the Island. major palmes was heare ffryday the .15. Thomas Averies 2 Calves were fetched whome the .22. wee gathered our peases Renolds had a wheather twelve shillings prise the .28. wee powned peases ffriday .29. saterday .30. mr Richardson shewed mee the letter dated .15. of July recevied it the night before sabath day .31. saterday 30 the meeting apoynted at my hous about benit deane & Richardson

The seventh moneth is september and hath .30. days monday the first and monday the 8. a meeting at Henrie Eli(o)ts house monday 15 wee wer at quaquatag Tusday the 16 a County Court at New london my wife was at Tagwonck the Rhod Island Cour(t) monday 22 william Jonson and Elizabeth badcock were maried our Calf was caried to leftenant masons monday .29. samuell is goeing to the bay: it is michelmas day

The .14. of December mosses Child was buried it was sabath day.

The Eight moneth is october hath .31. days wensday the first wensday the 8 day I was at Coneticut wensday .15. the .16. day I came whome the .17. day I shaked downe the aples wensday .22. I caried Captayne pendiltons booke whome samuell drove the steeres to Tho Avery wee had gathered all our aples the .27. day monday wee ffetched whome our Rames wensday .29. the .30 day I sould my oats to Jonathan perker ffriday the 31 The firkin of butter that Curtice had weighed .77. pound the first of November.

The ninth moneth is November and hath 30. days saterday the ffirst monday the 3d mansseh came heare: samuell went to the bay saterday the .8. day manaseth went whome sabath day the ninth day we had no sermon and saterday the .15. samuell came whome from bostowne: sabath day the .16. widow waler died wensday the .19. shee was buried saterday the 22 samuell was at New London monday 24. wee met at Colvers about Crarie Thursday .27 the meeting at mr Noyses hous Dimon bark was Cast away sabath day .30. the sacrament was administred

Received of william Clisbee 0-16-9
Received of mr moss -00-18-06

The tenth moneth is December and hath .31. days monday the ffirst: The .5. day I was at New london with my Hide wee had kild our Cow and .5. swine the .6. day we kild a sheep: the .8. day monday I payd .3. bushels of pease to mr Noyses towards the next yeares Rate by ould york I fecht 2 barels from steeven the 12 and 13. day we mad .3. barles of drinke: monday the 15. sam brought whome the sow & 5 piggs monday 22 manaseth was heare Ephraim and Joseph kiled theyr swine: 24. day manaseth went whome Thursday .25. Christmas day our Constables to be Chosen my wife verie sick Tusday the .30. wensday .31. the grate snow ffell

The leventh moneth is Januarie and hath .31. days Thursday the ffirst the .6. day we had Turneps at maynes wensday the 7th. a day of ffasting and prayer Through the whole Colony Thursday the .8. day the 10. day saterday I begun to thresh the .13. day I payd mr Noyse: 8 bushels of wheate Thursday the .15. the 20 day wee are to meet at mr Noyses the bretheren only that day I fell downe the stayers Thursday .22. Clark came 23 day I went for the young Hors Thursday .29. M. S.: R L: saterday .31. I went to see Ephraim that night mrs moss departed this life: sabath day the .8. of ffebruarie 1679-80 I begun with Carie latham

The Twelvth moneth is ffebruarie and hath .29. days: and sabath day the ffirst and sabath day the .8.

mr Noyse was at New london I Received peeter
Chocks leter the 9th day wee met at Robins Towne
sabath day the 15. the 16 samuell went to pachaug
my yong horse was Taken up the 14. day Valentines
day and sabath day the .22. the sacrament of the
Lords super administred the .25. day we were at mr
Noyses house sabath day the .29.

The .8. day of ffebruarie 1679:80 I begun the
yeare with Carie latham -†††††--------------------

The first moneth is march hath .31. days monday
the first and is the first yeare after the leap yeare and
the yeare of our lord 1680 monday the ffirst day the
.2d. day wee made an end of Threshing we had .56.
bushels of oats and monday the .8. wee Layd out the
Contrie high ways Thomas and Hanah was heare:
samuell mason had six shillings worth of Cider Tusday
the first day of Catachiseing at mr Noyses house the
.13. day monday the .15. I begun to garden: monday
.22. day twesday wee begun to sow wheat we met at
mr masons about goodwife Renolds and her Two
daughters Thursday .25. a greate snow mr Richardson Tould me that the Rhod Islanders were com to
run the Line it is Called our Lady day the same night
I aquainted mr sa(m) mason wensday .31. we are to
meet at mr masons house

The second moneth is April and hath .30. days the

first Thursday wee met at mr Noyses the .4th. day
sabath wee had a sacrament the .6. day Thomas &
Hanah went whome we began the ferry .7. day Ann
went to Hanahs Thursday the .8. sam cut his legg the
13. day Thursday the .15. it thundred and Rained it
was apoynted for to Chuse millitarie officers the 17.
day I made even with Renolds & moss only my Two
barles Thursday .22. a Trayning. 23d I entred into
72 our old spotted sow was lost Thursday .29. ffriday
30. wee had payd mr Noyse Three bushels of peas
Eight bushels of wheate five bushels of Indean Corne
the whole is ffiftie three shillings and six pence for
this yeare. 1680 : :

The third moneth is may .31. days the first saterday
the .3d day the soril mare ffolled saterday the .8. wee
were at Tagwonck monday the .10. I delivered ffouer
bushel of Indean corne to John ffrink for Agustine
williams the .11. day I am to set forth to the Court
saterday the .15. I was at Coneticot and saterday the
.22. I came whome : saterday .29. heare was Testimonys Taken monday 31. heare was more Testimonys
to be taken

The .23d. of June .1680 samuell stanton and boren-
del denison was maried

The .16. of June 1680. a day of humilliation
Through the Collony

The fouerth moneth is June hath .30. days the first Tusday County Court at New london Tusday the .8th. wensday the .9th. wee shore our sheep : the 14th. day samuell went to the bay Tusday the .15. I Received one bushell and halfe of oats of mr Richardson for atachment and other writings against June Court and one gallion of Cider Thursday the .17. I was at New london ffor mallases Tusday .22. mr Edward Randulph was heare wee wened our Calves : and Tusday .29. wensday the .30. wee put out .9. Calves 4. ours. 5 of samuels

The .21. of July 1680 : the marshall was heare and seased mr Joseph Clerke : :

The fift month is July hath .31. days the first Thursday The .8. day is Thursday a towne meeting to publish Court orders The .9th day a meeting at mr Noyses and Thomas Eemans Edwards was buried mr Richardson at Rhod Island the .15. Thursday wee were att Tagwonck: Saxstone was maried To the widow Cheesbrough Thursday the .22. a meeting at mr Noyses ould wheeller was there: Thursday .29. saterday .31. Renolds Abused in the Eevning by severall persons T. f: E B: E C:

28. of Agust .1680. Ephraims his .4th sonn was borne

The sixt moneth is Agust hath .31. days sabath day the first the 3d day wee had our wheate and oats in sabath day the Eight I was ill sabath day the .15. the .16. day our Rams was caried away samuel went to bostowne sabath day the .22. the 23. day Curtice was heare sabath day .29. Tusday .31. I was with all the sick folke Towards poquatuck

The 3d of september .1680. my soril horse died

The same day steeven Richardson was to go to Rhod Island

The seventh moneth is september 30 days the first wensday the 2 day Thursday wee blooded our horses mr Noyse was heare and Thursday I gathered our hops .T.G.1 was heare wensday 8 wensday the .15. the .16. day wee made Cider Tho Rose maried. John Ascraft buried and wensday .22. I was at poqunump and Tagwonck we had all our salt Hay whome wensday .29. Thursday the .30::

The .13. of october .1680. I received of william Clisbee one firkin: one pair of gloves .4. laces. one yard of cruel.

The Eight moneth is october hath .31. days the first friday Thomas Averie and his wife was heare ffryday the .8. I had shews of Thomas Rose wee gathered the aples of the litle orchard 20 bushels ffriday the .15. I was at new london had .28. yards of lining at £3–10s-

and 2 shillings in thread and ffriday 22. 23 I made an
end makeing of Cider the 25. Thomas and Hanah went
whome with theyr sope ffriday .29. I was at Clisbees '
and mill sabath day .31.

the 26 day of october .1680. samuells 2 men went
to Woodcocks hunting

The .28. day wee met at mr Noyses moses Captayne
pendilton John ffish Tho Minor

The ninth month is November hath 30. days the
first monday and monday the .8. day the .12. day
friday we brought whom our Rams monday the 15.
hanahs second sonn was borne and monday the 22
samuell sent his pork to New london wensday .24th.
day the marshall served the Execution on payns land
mr balden steeven Richardson swore prisors: 25.
Captayn denison took out Atachment against morse
and monday .29. samuell went to bostowne the .30th.
day there fell a greate snow

The last two weeks of November or about the 15
day & the begining of December the greate blase
was seen in the skie and Continued to the .15. or .16.
of Januarie

The tenth moneth is december hath .31. days the
first wensday and wensday the .8. the .10th. day
samuell came from bostowne the .11th. day Thomas.

Averie had away the white Cow the .12. day Josephs fouerth daughter was borne wensday the .15. a day of humiliation in The whole Colony wensday the .22. Thomas John and Christopher Avery was heare wee Tooke up the mares and Thursday the .23. a meeting at mr Noyses: saterday .25. and Christmas day the .26. day the Lords supper to be administred the .30. day a day of Choyse of Towne officers ffryday .31. I had been lame.

The leventh moneth is Januarie hath .31. days the first saterday and saterday the .8. sams Cow Calved and saterday the .15. I had been lame in my ffeet .3. weeks the .16. goodwife deane was p pounded to the Church the .17. day the Canoow went to New London Clement manaseth Hanah and Thomas Avery was heare The 20 day I began to thresh pease satterday .22. I was at samuell masons saterday .29. the .30. mr woodbrige Taught heare monday .31. Thomas Avery was heare::

The last of ffebruarie or the ffirst of march 1680-81 Ebenezer billings was to An Comstock maried

The twelvth month is Ffebruarie hath 28. days the first Tusday a verie wet day wensday the .2. sam went to boston the .6. manaseth cam hither Tusday the .8. a towne meeting warned on wensday Tusday the .15. manaseth was to go whome he wrought heare

8. days the .16. day manaseth went whome Tusday
.22. the Constables tooke theyr oath: monday the
.28. day wee payd goodman searles ffouer bushels of
Indean Corne .10. shillings

25. of march .1681. samuell tooke the plow lands
to sow out plow the halfes it being the lady day

The ffirst month is march and hath .31. days Tusday the ffirst the second after the leape yeare and the
yeare of our Lord .1681. and from the Creation
.5630. I had been very lame in my ffeet and hands
sabath day the .6. I was not at the meeting Tusday
the .8. day and Tusday the .15. York had atachment
monday the 21. sam was at New London Tusday .22.
sam Closed all acounts with Haris the .24. wee met
at mr Noyses in p peration to the sacrament: samuell
tooke all the Corne to sow and to plant to halfes for
this yeare the 25 of march: sabath day .27. the sacrament is to be administred Tusday the .29. Ephraim
and his wife was heare Thursday .31.

The second month is April and hath .30. days the
ffirst ffryday the C(h)urch met at mr Noyses about
mr Richardson and Mayne monday the .4th. the day
ffor Catekising of Children ffriday the .8th. day we
wer veiwing the tyd at mistick and the .11th. day
againe the .13. day apoynted to be a day of humillia-

tion ffriday the .15. samuell was at New london the
.18. day wee met at samuell masons ffriday .22. I
sowed the garden John Hartnes went to ffishers
Island saterday .23d I Entred into 73. yeares of my
age samuell came whome ffrom bostowne and ffriday
.29. our sister Chapman was heare and hanah saterday the 30 I had whome my new Cart from Ephraim

The .6. of may 1681 Joseph stantons second wife
was buried: the .8. day I received Brother Benjamin
his Letter from Antego.

The third moneth is may and hath .31. days the
ffirst is sabath day & sabath day The .8. the .9th.
day my wife went to see goodwife Holmes the .10.
day wee went to halehage sabath day the .15. the .16.
day I was to see Jonathan Avery the .17. day I shot
the boards and sabath day 22. 23 I was at New
london ffor malasses. I caried the Contribusion for
Condy and sabath day the .29. monday the .30th.
samuell drove .12. Catle to Narraganset Thomas Edwards wife brought thither Two black piggs Tusday
the .31.

mrs Noyse is to goe to bostowne June the .13th.
1681.

The ffouerth moneth is June and hath .30. days
the ffirst is wensday and Tusday the .7th. wee were

at yeomans wensday the .8. day wee shore our
sheep I was at the Court: wensday the .15. a day of
humiliation The .16. a meeting at mr Noyses house
wensday .22. the .21. samuel came from mr smiths
Thursday .23. my wife was at Thomas Averys: the
.27. I was at Clements. 28. my wife ffell out of the
Canoow: wensday .29. I and my wife went to mill
Thursday the .30. my wife very sick mr Jeremie
Hobart came to Daniell Masons house

about the .10th. of Agust .1681 Benjamin palmer
brought whome his wife

The fift moneth is July and hath .31. days the
ffirst is ffryday the fift day is Tusday: Clements second wife died our daughters in law was heare and
hanah and her husband and Children the .8. day
hanah went whome Joseph and Samuell gon to New
london ffryday and ffryday the .15. samuell is gon to
bostowne the .16. day the sun apeared very strang
and pale ffryday .22. sam Came from bostowne I was
at mr Noyses and at Ephraim and Josephs and ffriday 29. we had into the barne .4. loads of oats 2. of
of wheate. one of pease the 30 day I was at Crandalls
mill sabath day the .31:

The sixt moneth is Agust and hath .31. days the
ffirst is monday our Three Rams and one yew was

Caried away my wife went to Tagwonck the .8. day
monday goo(d) wife springer had the .3. piggs: the
.11. & the .12th days the Elders were heare and
monday the .15. Samuel was in the bay the .18 a
generall day of humilliation the .19. day it Rayned
and samuell came whome monday .22. Tusday .23. I
was at Crandals mill: Thursday .25. John ffish and
Hanah steere was maried: and monday .29. at mill:
Tusday 30 sam drove home Thomas Averies yearelings
wensday .31.

The seventh month is september and hath .30. days
the ffirst is Thursday wensday the .7. Thursday the
.8. day samuell bought benits horse marie Lord was
heare The .9. day samuell went to New London
Thursday the .15. Jonathan Avery was buried: Thursday .22. I was at new London Court monday .26. wee
began to make Cider: we had Two Cow Calves Killed
and Thursday .29. the ffreemen were to Chuse deputies
ffriday .30:

The .18. day of this october .1681. william marsh
was maried and Elizabeth yeomans the same day
Joseph came to learne to write

The eight moneth is october and hath .31. days the
ffirst is saterday and saterday the .8. sabath the .9.
mr Noyse at New london monday .10. I caried .2.

bushells of Corne to goodman searles Tusday the .11. Joseph and I was to Renew our bounds of our .100. ackers: and saterday the .15. I was at Tagwounck I had made a end of poundig of Cider saterday .22. I sould my bull to Thomas Rose the .27. I was at new London and toke pay for my bull: munday the 31. mr Noyse was goeing to the bay Thomas Averie was heare:: Joseph left of writeing heare:: the 14. day of November 1681

The Ninth moneth is November and hath .30. days the ffirst is Tusday and Tusday the .8. day hanah was heare and: Ephraims wife:: it was the first snow The 10th. day: a Train(in)g day: Tusday the 15. wensday the .16. a day of thausgiveing through the whole Collony and very wet: 21. day monday samuell went to the bay: Tusday 22. I was at mill mr Noyse was com whome Tusday the 29 wensday the .30. samuell went to the bay with horses Thomas and his wife and Children were heare:

The Tenth moneth is december and hath .31. days the ffirst is Thursday the .6. day I went to the widow Haris the .8th. day Thursday the .9th. day I came whome ffrom Naraganset: Thursday the 15. manaseth Minor and his wife and Two Daughters were heare: samuell and marie Lord was maried at mr Noyses house Thursday the .22. a meeting at mr Noyses 23d we Chose Towne officers sabath day .25. and Christmas day John minor was heare and marie minor the 28 day Joseph wells was maried & Hanah Renolds were maried Thursday 29: we were about the ministrie land & 30 day John and marie went whome satterday the .31.

The eleventh moneth is Januarie and hath .31. days the ffirst is sabath day the .7th. day I made an End threshing of samuells wheate sabath day the .8. day the 14 day gershum palmer and Elis aprhended sabath day .15. benit and his wife was prayed for: and sabath day the 22. Tusday 24. I was at mill I made an end threshing of samuels oats mr piggen was heare and Joseph wels sabath day .29. the 30 day I begun to Thresh wheate that was betwixt us Tusday 31. Joseph was sicke the 5 of ffebruarie 1681–2.

The Twelvth moneth is ffebruarie and hath .28. days the ffirst is wensday Thursday Candilmas day the Lectter at mr Noyses: the third day I branded horses at galops John start had Two gallions of Cider Tusday the .7. the Church met at mr noyses wensday the .8. day sam drove away the steeres the .14. day I had threshed the pease voletines day wensday the .15. I begun to thresh the oats between us: my wife was verie il: Tu(s)day .21. the Church met about goodwife deane wensday .22. my wife was sick Joseph was heare

Tusday .23.: The ffirst of march 1681–2 major palmes weere heare

The ffirst moneth is march hath .31. days the ffirst is wensday the yeare .1682. the third yeare after the Leap yeare : the .2d. thursday the Lecture at mr Noyses. wensday the .8. samuel was com from mr smiths Thursday the 9th. I was at New london with piggen wensday the .15. I was at Thomas Edwards quinameset kiled a wolfe the .21. I sowed wheate wensday the .22. and wensday 29. I made an End of sowing of oats. mr Noyse was heare the .30. day my wife tooke phisicke. Joseph was heare ffriday the 31:: the .6. day of Aprile Ephraim brought his Catle .1682

The second moneth is April hath .30. days. the ffirst is saterday samuell at New London my wife Tooke phisiuqe the 2d day Captayne averie was heare the .6. day the lecter the .7. day I sowed garden saterday the 8 day the 10 day a trayneing saterday the 15. I rode young horse to the Meeting the .16. day mrs noyse was delivered the .18. day the .20. day we met at Steephen richsons saterday the .22. day we lost 3 lams with the storme saterday .22.

sabath day the 23. I begun my .74. yeare of my age
sabath day the .30th we had five Children baptized
by mr Noyse 2 John gallops .2. of peter Crarie and
one moses palmers.

The third moneth is may hath .31. days the ffirst
is monday Thursday the 4th day the lecter was at
Ephraims house the 7th day the sacrament was administred the Indean died monday the .8th day tusday the .9th. wee caried muck and monday the .15.
day the .19. day we wer veiwing Elihue his land
monday .22. samuell went to bostowne the .25. a day
of humilliation the .26. day samuell came whome
monday .29. samuell took the .5. Cows for .£5 in
buter and cheese wensday the .31. we caried ann to
hanah

The third of June 1682. samuell ffetched Captayne
denison bull. we turned out 6 calves and one yeareling three of mine calves

The ffouerth month is June hath .30. days the ffirst
is thursday the second day we shore our sheep. the
.6. day I went to Court samuell and his wife to Coneticut the .8. day thursday I came whome the .9. day
the bees swarmed Thursday the 15 the .16. day I
planted Cabeges it was wet the .21. day the white
Cow Calved Thursday the 22. samuell went to hart-

ford with the Canoow my wife was sick: wensday
.28. samuell masons youngest daughter died Two in
daughters within one weeke died and Thursday the
.29. samuell came whome ffrom Coneticut it was
verie wet and ffriday the .30. the .29. day mercie
and An begun to goe to goodman searls

The fift moneth is July hath .31. days the ffirst is
saterday and saterday the .8. I was at Thomas Edwards I sowed turneps in the playne the .6. Children
went to Tagwonck: saterday the .15. sams Trop
Cheched a wolfe. I fetched .4. loads of wood saterday the .22. I came ffrom mr withrels the .14. day of
sams sicknes: 28. day Clement and manaseth Reaped
wheat we had between us .49. shock of wheate saterday .29. monday .31.

wensday the second of Agust 1682. quinemeset
agreed to worke .2. moneth with me for Twentie
shillings to be payd in mony when steeven Richardson pays mee

The sixt moneth is Agust hath .31 days the ffirst
is Tusday wee had all our oates in Tho .8. Tusday
wee were at gallops and wensday the .9th. Clement
& manaseth went whome I was at mill manaseth had
sams hat the .14. day the Indean was taken up mr
John Richardson was heare Tusday the .15. the .16.

day the blasing star first apeared the .18. day I sould
my Catle to John Babcock the .19. day the Rams was
caried to the Island Tusday .22. the .24. day Captayn
Averie and his wife was heare 27. day mr John
Richardson taught major winthroup fecth his horses
mr Noys was heare Thursday .31. last mowed

The seventh moneth is september hath .30 days the
ffirst is ffryday we had all our hay whome the .7. day
I was at Crandals mill ffriday the .8th the .14. day
was a ffast at mr Noyse his house ffriday .15. ffriday
22. I was at Court ffriday .29. and mickelmas day
saterday the .30. I ffetched whome all marahs Corne
out of the playne

The second of october .1682. Tho: Averys daughter
was borne

The Eight moneth is october. hath .31. days the
ffirst is sabath day the sixt day wee had in al our
Corne Joseph had the Cart away and sabath day the
.8. sabath day the .15. I was at bostowne and saterday .21. I cam-e whome sabath day .22. and sabath
day the .29. mr baylie Taught at stonenigton and
Tusday the .31.

The .7th. of December .1682. I caried my hide to
Thomas Rose 8 s due. The .21. of october 1682.

Clement and manaseth was both heare the 20 of november Clisbee one s.-6 d: John Renolds 3 shillings

The ninth moneth is November hath .30. days the ffirst is wednesday a day of publick Thankesgiveing sabath day the .5. wee had no meeting wensday the .8. I was at New london for my Chest the .10th. day I ffetched whome the Ram wensday the .15. I had Corne of queoducks the 16 day I was at Ephraims and Joseph wensday the .22. the 20. day I was at Cales wensday 29. thursday the 30 a meeting to be at mr Noyses house mistris wels admited to pertake with the Church

The tenth moneth is December .31. days the first ffriday the third sabath day the lords super administred friday the .8. sabath day the .10th. mr Noyse came not to the meeting monday the .11. I ffetched the swine whome ffriday the .15. and ffriday the .22. I brought whome the steere ffryday .29. we had all our Catle whome and mr Noyse was heare: and manaseth sabath day .31. 26 day we Chose Constables marah was published.

The eleventh month is Januarie hath .31. days the ffirst is monday I begun to Thresh marath went to Holmes monday the .8. Thomas Avery was heare and his wife Deborah ffrinke went whome Joseph pem-

erton brought marah hither monday the .15. the
.16. day I was at poquatuck to see marah thursday
the 18. day it was wet monday .22. monday 29. I
branded Colts at gallops 30 we were at witers .31. we
Examined Henrie steveens prentice his ffather Ref-
fused to let him goe with his. master and sayd he
would resist his master and the Com r s too and toke
him by the hand and held him

The Twelvth moneth is ffebruarie hath .28. days
the ffirst is Thursday wee were at mr Noyses in
pr paration to the sacrament the .4th. day we had the
lords super the .7th. day Ephraim Joseph and Elis
was heare Thursday .8. day and Thursday .15. the
.19. day I made an End winowing of oates we had
.41. bushells and marah .47. and an halfe Thursday
22 I was at Tho Averies samuell was sick saterday
.24. I was at mill wensday the 28 day

The 29. of march 1683 I was at Joseph pemertons

The ffirst moneth is march hath ·31. days Thursday
the ffirst ffrom the Creation .5632. and leap yeare 1
day I ffetche(d) whome my plow the yeare of our Lord
.1683. and Thursday the .8. day I was at the mill and
maried John bolten Rezident in stoneington and sarah
Cheesbrough of the same Towne major winthroup
was at mistick the .15. day I maried John Holam
Reziding in stoneington and prudence Richardson of

the same Towne: the .19th. day Joseph pemerton now
Reziding in stoneington and the widow marah minor
were maried: the 20th. day a deep snow wensday .21.
manaseh came hither Thursday .22. ffriday .23.
Joseph and marah pemerton went away ffriday 30.
manaseth and his ffamily came hither Thomas Rose
brought mee Two paier of shews saterday 31

The second month is Aprill hath .30. days sabath
day the ffirst saterday the .7th. I made an End sowing
of wheate and oats sabath day the .8. we had the
sacrament of the Lords super Thursday the .12. day
I payd my Contrie Rate 2 bushels of wheate five pecks
and halfe of Indean Corne at .00-11-02. the same day
I was at mill and Elnathan sabath day the .15. the
.16. day Clement and Hanah was heare I was at our
daughter pembertons with my letter and sabath day
.22. the 23. manaseth begun to plow ffor Indean Corne
in the playne the .26. day the Church met at the
meeting house about an agreement to Renew our
Covenant and Concerning the Children of the Church
to apeare at som time apoynted by mr Noyse to dis-
course with him that he might be satisfied of theyr
knowledg that is to say all adult persons maried at
one time: and unmaried at another: also concerning
goodwife deane her acknowledgment: whether searles

and his wife did sufficiently prove the mater: 28 day
I was at Thomases monday 30

The third moneth is may hath .31. days Tusday the
ffirst the .7th. day I was at mr Noyses the .8th. day
Tusday I sowd parsneps in the garden manaseth
plowed for semunt the .13th. day Hope Chapman and
martha queenbee were published the .15. day is Tusday John came heare and Tusday .22. 23d I was at
New London John went home I gave my Testimony
Concering mr Blindmans letter that he had received
his pay ffrom mr Christohers by bils of Exchang from
newfoundland by Hopkins and lane: I delivered to
mr plum 4 shillings ffor John birchard merit Hue
huberd widow waterhous being pr sent monday .28.
I was at Thomas Averys and my wife Tusday .29.
wensday .30. wee shore some sheep Thursday .31. a
day of humilyation

The ffouerth moneth is June hath 30 days ffriday
the ffirst I reckned with Henrie steephens due 4.s
the 6 day John Coale and his wife was Examined
ffriday the .8th. the .11th. day I Cleaved Clobords
and was at mill the 13. day Clements mare was
buried the 14. day I was at the saw mill ffryday the
.15. manaseth dresed Clapboardes the .18 day Joseph
brought hither his Calves. the .21. day Hanah was
heare and fryday .22. the 28. day manaseth was at

New london ffriday .29. wee began to mow and saterday the 30:

The .2d. day of July Ebinezer Billings brought
whome my Two horses and took 4 1 of woole ffor his
labour

The ffift moneth is July hath 31 days sabath day
the ffirst and the second day monday I caried mr
Noyses firkin of buter came to 80 pound the firkin
weighed .13.1 so there remained .10 shillings to me
sabath day the .8. the sacrament was administred
monday the .9th. quinameset began his .20. days for
a Coate and sabath day the .15. ffryday the .20th
wee began to Reape wheate and sabath day .22. monday 23. wee had 400 sheaves of wheate ffriday I was
visiting the sick and sabath day .29. Tusday 31

wensday the .8th. of Agust 1683. I and manaseth
begun with hugh hubberd to fferie+-------------------

The sixth moneth is Agust bath .31. days wensday
the ffirst my wife went to Hanahs mr Richardson
sent ffor mee sabath day the ffift about one a clok in
that mr Richardson departed this life the .8th. day
A day of humillation I was at New london monday
the .13. a greate storme that blasted all the Trees
wensday the 15. ffryday the .17. Thomas Ave(r)y his

wife and Children was heare mistris Richardson
made her will The 15 wensday: 21 Tusday I was at
Naraganset wensday 22 ffriday 24 I came whome
Thursday the .30 I was taken sick and continued so
Eight weekes and was wholy lost

The seventh moneth september hath 30 days saturday the ffirst

The second day of Januarie 1683–4 I branded a
black horse Colt on the neare shoulder thus K on the
neare buttuck thus ᴛ_M he have a halpenie cut on the
ffore side of Each Eare The same day I branded A
bay horse Colt on the neare shoulder thus K and on
the neare buttuck thus ᴛ_M he had a halpenie cut on the
ffore side of Each Eare he is a naturall pacer

The Eight moneth is october hath 31 days monday
the ffirst The .28. day of this moneth was the ffirst
time I came to the meeting house.

The .10th. day of November 1683. James yorke
senior was buried

The ninth moneth is November hath 30 days Thursday the ffirst and sabath day the .4th. mr okes
preached at stoneington and Thursday the .8. hanah
fetched her sheep the 9. day and Ephraim and Joseph
brought the .32. pound of lead we had .42. sheep this
9th day the 12 day monday we ffecthed 4 bushells of

Turneps at gershum palmers and Thursday the .15. I
was at mil the 16 day we killed our swine Thursday
22. the 25 day we had A Sacr(a)ment I was sick

The tenth moneth is december hath .31. days saterday the ffirst this weeke John and Thomas minor wer
heare with us saterday .8. they went both away this
weeke there was A Court at New London the .8. day
at Night Cristopher Avery died it being saterday and
saterday the .15. Thomas Avery was heare the 16 day
I was at meeting the 18 day manaseth killed the pide
bull saterday the 22. I delivred simun the .15. shillings of mony and goodman deane was heare The .28
day Josephs third sonn was borne saterday the 29th
day Thomas Avery and his wife and theyr Two Children went whome monday 31:

The eleventh moneth is Januarie hath 31. days
Tusday the ffirst we winowed ffive bushels and three
pecks of wheate and tusday the .8. I made an End of
Threshing my wheate the 15 day I made an End
Threshing of manaseth barly tusday the 22 we had
about 12 bushels of wheate Tusday .29. Thursday .31.
I begun to Thresh Christmas Eve and Ended shrove
Tusday

The Twelvth month is ffebruarie hath .29. days
ffryday the ffirst and is leape yeare the yeare of our
Lord .1683. and Tusday the .5. and shrove Tusday

and ffriday the 8 the .9th. day manaseth went to mr
Holam to Carie barels the 14 day Thomas Avery and
his wife was heare ffriday the 15 manaseth ended
Ephraims Cloth we had Tenn or eleven lambs Thursday 21 I payd the deacon ffriday 22 saterday I was at
Thomas Averys sabath day .24. we had the lords
super administred and 28 I was at Thomas Rose
Thomas Avery and his wife was heare ffriday 29 we
wer about the brigg this was leap yeare The 16 day
of mar 1683.-4 gabril Harice departed this life

The ffirst moneth is march and have 31. saterday
the ffirst the yeare 1684. and the first yeare after the
leap yeare ffrom the Creation 5633 the ffirst day verie
wet the 3 day the 11 day I was at mile it was Tusday
and saterday the 15 the 17 day my wife and I were
at the widow yorks the Children were CatteChized by
mr Noyse saturday the .22. Joseph his Catle went
whome it was a greate storme saterday 29 sabath
day 30 we had the sacrament administred Captayne
Denison p taked with us the 31 day we sowed sams
ffeild to wheate litle Clement whome with his mare

April is the second moneth and hath 30 days
Tusday the ffirst Tusday the .8. the 13 day sabath day
the 14 day our Canoow went to New london with 30
bushels of oates Tusday the 15 day the S. M. Y.
I sowed nine bushels of oates Tusday 22 wensday .23.

the first day of my .76. of my age the last night a
great storme and A high Tide wensday the 30 it
thundred and was a storme

The .2d. of may was our day to Chuse deputies

The .7. day of may 1684 mistris willet died and
was buried

May is the third moneth and hath 31 days Thursday the ffirst Thursday the .8. day and Thursd(ay)
the .15. day the .16. day the white faced mare had a
bay mare Colt a black Tayle and a black mane and
Thursday the 22. I was at mr Noyses the 23. my wife
went to Hanah Thursday the 29. ffryday 30. Thomas
Avery his wife and Children wer heare mr John
Richardson sent for mee saterday 31 I was at mr
Noyses

Thurs(d)ay the 5 of June mr Noyse and his wife
went forth for bostowne and Newberie

June is the fouerth moneth hath 30 days sabath day
the ffirst the sixt day of June wee had .37. sheep
shorne Thomas Avery and his wife and Children was
heare the 11 day mr John Richardson taught heare
the 12 day John Smith and marie minor was heare and
sabath day the 15 the .20. day I was at Thomas Avery
and sabath day the .22. day and s(a)bath day .29.
monday 30 I and moses palmer and Ephraim minor

was renewing the bounds of Elihue Cheesbroh six hundred ackers of land at the mill brooke 300: at Tagwonck: 300 and found all the Trees mentioned on the writing mentioned

July is the ffift month hath 31 days Tusday the ffirst and the second day we had seven Calves to Tagwonck and Tusday the .8. the 13 day the sacrament was administred goodman searles was admonished Tusday the .15. we had 5. mowers Tusday .22. the .23. day we made our ffirst Reek of hay the 24 day verie wet Tusday 29 Thursday 31 wee had 15 Loads of hay whome.

The sixt month is Agust and hath 31 days ffriday the ffirst ffriday .8. day our Calves were brought whome the same day my wives mare had Colt the .9. day ffrink had his horse away manaseh was sick: Tusday the 12. Thomas avery his Childe was buried ffriday the .15. we Ca(r)ied our Rams to the Iland and wensday .20. our Rams came whome my wife was at Tagwonck ffriday 22 . ffriday .29. the 30 day my wife went to hanah sabath day .31.

The seventh moneth is september and hath 30 days monday the ffirst monday the 8 ffriday the .12. manaseth tooke phisiquek he was very sick monday the .15. Thomas avery sent phisick saterday the .20 my wife was very sick and monday .22. we Tooke up our salt hay and monday .29. and miche(1)mus day the .30th. day I was taken ill on my back my wife ile : manaseth pounded aples mr masons horses in the Corne ffeild

The Eight month is october and hath 31 days wensday the ffirst sabath day the .5. we had the sacrament: wensday the 8 day we gathered our Corne the .9. day we had it in the house the .15. day wensday we had all our Corne in: mr Noyse was heare wensday the .22. a day of humileiation Through the .3. Colonies Reckned with mr Noyse and payd my owne Rate and manases: 1-16s: the firkin of buter came to 1-11-00. wensday 29. we had all our yards Cleared the same time we had all our Catle whome but one yearleing ffriday the .31. and wet

The ninth moneth is November and hath 30 days saterday the ffirst and wensday the .5. a day of thankesgiveing throughout the Colonie the .6. day manaseth went to bostowne saterday the .8. I was at hanas and saterday the .15 the 18 day we had our swine whome and saterday 22 Tho: averie went whome with theyr Children 25 day A snow our Canoow was driven away and saterday .29. sabath day the 30 we had the sacrament administred

The tenth moneth is december and hath 31 days

monday the ffirst we kild our steere and bull and
swine wensday the 3d day I Recconed with Tho Rose
and ballanced at acounts between him and mee: and
monday the 8. day manaseth helped Ephraim and
monday the .15. Joseph was heare and monday the
.22. Thursday the .25. and Christmas day and
apoynted to Chuse Constables and other officers monday 29. wensday .31. manaseth was at the smiths

The .8. day of Januarie 1684. at Ephraim minors
mr Noyse warned the Church to Cleare their acounts
with the deackon by that day month or otherwise to
be dealt with all if not done

The eleventh moneth is Januarie and hath 31 days
Thursday the ffirst and thursday the .8. the Church
met at Ephraim minors house and sabath day the .11.
the Lords super is to be administred the 13 & 14
days verie Cold Thursday the .15. the .17. day Joseph
minor Returned to New london the .18. day at night
a greate storme Thursday the .22. Joseph was heare
I had in three days cut 100. stakes the .26. day we
had 3 Calves the .27. day my wife and I was at Tagwonck and hanah was heare the .29. day Thursday
saterday .31. we had 14. lambs: the 29. day I cared
goodman searles Two bushels of oats

The Twelvth moneth is ffebruarie and hath 28 days
sabath day the ffirst and sabath day the .8. and

sab(a)th day the .15. the 17 day it was wet manaseth went to looke the wolfe and the .20. day I went
to see litle Ephraim his Eie that was hurt sabath day
the .22. my wife was very sick saterday the 28 day
wet and snow

Thursday the .26. of ffebruarie 1684-5 there was
A Church meeting at Nehemiah palmers house

———

NOTE—The following entries were made in the
diary at various times by Thomas Minor.

———

Delivered unto poor man mine (torn) A horse that
he bout of mister Richisoone and by his apointment
and order a horse a chesnute Culer with a blase in his
face one croped Eare and some white about his
nose galed with a halter the crop beinge on the left
eare and in my presants marked withe a T on the
Left foote afor I Say by mee delivered this 14 day
of aguste 1661 with my hand

This horse was   Richard Smith
delivered in our
presents as witnes
our hands

   Thomas Minor Ju(n)ier
   Ephraim minor

The 20th of october being Tusday 1663 hanah Avery & her mother Tould us that shee had entertained Samuell Roice againe Ever since that night that I sould my Cow to philipes at Carie lathams

+

Y WP: 1 : 2 : 34

the Chest

T: M—

shipped by the grace of god in good order and well Conditioned by me: peeter Olliver of bostowne for the proper acounte and adventure of walter palmer: in and upon the good ship Called the speedwell: whereof is master under god for this pr sent voyage David avecrumb: and now riding at anchor in the harbor of bostowne: and by gods grace bound for new london or pecot (Pequot) to say one: hh: two barels with salt and goods: one chest with goods two bras ketles with an old sayle in one of them and five siths with other goods: being marked and numbred as in the margent and are to be delivered in the like good order and well conditioned at the aforesaid port of new london or pecot the danger of the seas only excepted unto me John Tinker or to his assignes he or they paing fraight for the said goods after the rate of thirtie shillings p tun: In witnes whereof the master or purser of the said ship hath affirmed to three bils of lading all of this tenour and date the one

of which three bills being acomplished the other two
to stand void: and so god send the good ship to her
desired port in safety amen this .8. of november:
1660: .: dated in Boston.

David avecrumb

The 8th. of februarie 1661 I went To speake with
a frend: but found I none: this is the second time I
tried a man: but I wile for beare the third if that I
can: the first he witnessed with a Rattan the second
he turned me of with a slam: oh the 22 of July 1662
what biter Curses from him did I heare pray god to
keep me in thy feare:

The 16. day of Januarie 1664 The Constable and
the Townesmen wer apointed to Take the lists and
p fit them and make the Rate for the Contrie 30 £:
The same day I was p mised our 300. ackers of land:
The first of march

The 22 of october 1662. Tho stafford his request
to remember him 20 shilling upon half his acount
wt any of the undertakers or myselve

The 21. of Agust 1663 Aron start tould us that
about yt day .5. weeks before the Captayne Denison
said it was no matter though I did build I might do
what I would at tagwouncke I should never enjoy it
for it was the Coledges land it was about the 15 or

16. of July this was spoken: Jo: fish: Aron stark: at morgans.

The 22. of July 1662. its the day wherein I went astray in Companie of Two: yt p fessed they loved me well: but should we all hold on: I feare not only I but all had fell: my Children when I am dead: let none els but your selves This reade: but do take heed of being with your p fessed frends misled: the two Il nam to you: remember well the time and you will finde it true: Thomas Stanton and William Cheesbrough (names in cipher) wer the men: but I with them at: shas was meerly chatched then: oh lord deliver and keep: both me: and you: from our Corupt harts and them: and so I say amen

The 10 of June 1662 The acounte yt I cast up about the mares.

I paid to the Indeans & samuell wilson upon this acounte –04–19–06

at the Trading house my wife was
    in going and coming and all
    19 days & an hors 02– 07– 06
for Thomas going & in his sick-
    ness 20 days....... .... 02– 00– 00
myselve 14 days and our horse..... 02– 02– 00
my son Ephraim & his horse .2.
    days .... 00–:06 :00

my selve & sons riding to looke
 these mares 20. days & od..... 03 :00 :00
All Charges to the doctor from
 Rod Iland & the boate & other
 exspences at narraganset came
 to neer about thirteen pounds.. 13 :06 :00
for the mare that is wanting and to
 me & my wife & son the man
 that was with us Ruben willis
 detaning of my mares from
 me the hiding & Ridinge I
 shall intreate Counsell & advice
 and Rest

   Thomas minor
 all the Charges laid out it...... 28 :01 :00
 besides The mares
 More aded the 24th of June
 1662.. .... 3 : 8 : 0
       ————————
       31 : 9 : 0

Captaine denison for three Judgments writing for
John Borden demands .3 shillings a Judgment that is
.9 shillings & for fouer Testimonies & three actions
Entring twelve shillings to be paid to goodman
Rodgers upon the Captains acount
This 28 of march 1662 John borden

The .5th. of may .1675. samuel mason died being scalled to death

The .25. of may .1681 we put fforth 4. yearlings one Red Kow yeareling the 2. bulls one black cow on(e) with a litle whit upon the Tayle sum whit on the ffore Leg one smalle 2. yeare ould with a whit Tayl the rest black and one three yeare ould a black one with a whit Tayle

The .30th. of may .1681 samuell drove .7. Catl of mine to Narraganset Namely Three steers of three yeares ould and Three steers of Two yeares ould and one yeareling of one yeare ould a white one with Red Eares and Red spots about the head:

The .13. of may .1682. we put out .3. of 2 years old and 3 yearelings and samuell put out .9. Catle

: of Agust 1662. I & my (wife) dreamed at one time my wife dreamed that I struck her & said that I strucke at a dogg & I dreamed that I was going by a red   which had a puppie and shee bit at me & I struck her & struck my wife in the face either with my hand or fist which waked my wife & shee waked me & asked me what I did doe:

The 13. of may 1664. the originall Bound Tree marked in a litell swamp: on the west side of the Creek between the major mason and Carie latham

being a great Beech tree marked by Thomas minor
and Robert hempsteed being apointed thereunto: and
Captaine denison a witnes with us: was burned
downe and Aron start senior and John gallop senior
did both goe with me and see it did say in my hear-
ing that washam did it the 6 day of the week

The 14 of december 1662 the Capta Denison begun
to teache & Reade The 3 & 4 Chapters of James &
the 3 of Titus

The 21 I spake from the first of Esay after I spake
from the 17th of Jerimie

The 29th of march 1663. th(e) Captaine he tooke
mr stanton his turn and Reade the 31 psalme:

november 28 1666 The meeting was at mr Richersons it was wensday Thursday 29 we made the writing between The Towne & mr noyce There was a
towne meeting agreed upon to be the wensday ffollowing being the 5 of desember for to confirme the
agreement with mr noyes & about Cowsatuck and to
debate ffurther about the list

The first of Aprill being wensday the bay mare of
paines folled: 1663. a horse Colt 2 wale eies 4 whit
feet a whit face one black hoofe on the right feet
Thursday the 16 our bay mare brought a bay mare

Coult with the Right hoofe and foote behinde white
and a litell star in the forehead just above the twist
of the eare.

About the 22 of may 1663 the ould mare brought
a mare Coult with whit face and fouer whit feet we
eare marked hir the 30th of may

The 5th of June Josepth came whome with the
blacke mare and a Coult with a white blase in the face
turning to the right side above the eie the nose white
between the nostrills the uper lip white an horse and
a white hoofe on the felt foote behinde and the right
foot before half the hoofe whit and on the outside

The .6. day of June I found the Rone mare and a
blacke mare Coult with a litle white spot in the forehead

The 19th. of July being satterday 1662. Clement
and sarah waklin met me & my wife at new london

sarah waklin have had silke & lace of
    Joshua Raimond......................0 : 3 : 0
halfe one yard of penistone of picket
    that come to.......... ....0 : 2 : 6
one paier of shews..........................0 : 5 : 0
& fouer Cheeses ....— : — : —
Richard dart...................... ... .0 : 4 : 6

The .3. of may 1663 being sabath day the Roane mare and her yearling was seen heare by the house

The 18th day of June 1663 I found the 2 year ould bay mare with a stone coult: bay and a star in the fore head he hath his Taile doct

The 25 & 26 of februarie 1661 There was a Courte at shas about John mores

The 29 of Aprile 1662 we had a Courte at shas Concerning Captaine denison and mr Thomson

June the 27 1662 we had a Court at shas about Richard dart and The Indeans 4 actions.

The 24th. of februarie being Tusday There was a Courte at southertowne about Babcocke & mr stanton

william Dimocke store house at the Barbades

The 8 of July 1663 samuel Cheesbrough came to my house and brought an Execution for £2-2s I denied to deliver him any thing or to show him any thing and tould him that he should Carrie nothing of myne out of the house if I could well help it and that I did not owne him to be a constable to me at this time

The second of november 1663 manaseth begun his time with Richard dart for 2 years

The 25th of Agust 1663 being tusday there was a
Courte at shas Wequach Cooke was fined 62. fathom
for goeing to Coneticut to Complaine against Captaine
Denison as I was tould by an Indean Agedouset &
that Captaine Denison demanded Two fathome a
man of the pequit Indeans

To the Constable of southertowne or his deputie:
you are hear by requiered in his magesties name to
levy one to goods and Chattels of Thomas minor to
the value of Two pounds and deliver the same with
two shillings for this Execution to Thomas sha and
it is in sattisfaction of a Judgment granted by and
from the Courte of Comissionnors in southertowne.
  ˙ The last december: heareof faile not dated in southertowne This 30th of June 1663

By the Court

George denison

Clerke

This is a true Coppie of the Execution witnes my
haud   Samuel Cheesbrough

The 14. of march .1663. leent.   smith Thomas
lenards and John Els: Rune away

The .22. of march 1663-64 I rune the length of
James yorks land and found it +Twelve score pole
And the breadth and found it nine score pole at the

uper end from one corner Tree to the other as york
and his son shewed them to me and desired me to
measuer it

The .23. of march I was informed by H: g: that
Capt george Denison and James morgan upon the
.22. of march being Tusday 1663-64 was laing out of
land at misticke for Thomas parke Edmund faning
and Nathaniell Bebe: and allso that mr Buckley
would be at the fast at R: h: his house and would be
helpful to gather a H after the pr sbeteriall way: 24
day march

The 29 of Aprile 1664 Edmund ffainings Daughter
was drowned and buried the 30

The Commissionors meet allwaies on the first
Thursday of september

The 4th of ffebruarie mr perke departed this life
and was buried the 7th day being Tusday in the
yeare 1664

The 5th. of september 1665 our Brother Elihu
palmer died

The 26th. of october .1681. I Thomas minor: sould
to steeven Richardson of stoneington Eight barles of
Cider at ffouerteen shillings per barle to be payd in

mony ffive pounds Twelve shillings the Next Spring
my wife Joseph minor Junior samuell minor pr sent

The 27. of Aprile The Dun mare Brought an horse
Colt Bay with a Black mane a black list on the back
a black Taile the right foot behinde white a whit
hoofe a whit spot one the right side of the Twist of the
forehead thus D

The 14 day of May 1664 being saterday I found
the Roane mare with a blacke horse Coult and yeare
marked him The 27 of may I found the ould mare
with a Red mare Coult and a blacke mane

The .26. of march 1680 my wifes mare ffolled

(Torn out). . . of may 1667 my wives (torn out)
brought A mare Coult with A (torn out) the fforehead & one whit foot on the neer side behind & sume
part of she same foot the hoofe was whit & A blacke
mane

The .9th. of June .1667. being sabath day william
Cheesbroough departed this life and was Buried the
.11th day at weequataquock

saterday the 13 of July 1667 mr stantons man
daniell died in the night sudenly

The 17 of June 1667 (torn out) blacke Cow of (torn
out) williamson shee had the Two hinder ffeet whit &

the Top of the Taile white & a white udder shee was crop(ed) on the Right Eare an hollow crop or a peece cut out & (torn out) was delivered before goodwife gallop & my son Ephraim minor it being monday & the 2d day of the week

The 15th of July .1667. I delivered the blacke horse To Jerimie Bull at his house for Josepth as Atests Thomas: minor

Tusday 26. of november 1667. John Denison was maried brother gershom palmer The same week

Every ffouerth yeare is leape yeare Three years goe Cleare and the 4th is leape yeare the yeare .1666. is the Third yeare after the leape year and from the Creation .5615. and the .18. yeare of the Rainge of our sovereing lord king Charles the second

The yeare 1667. is the yeare 19. of the Reinge of our sovereinge lord king Charles the second

The .10th. of may .1684. wee put upon the Comon one Red steer 3 yeare old: 2 steeres of .2. yeares old .1. browne: one with a white back 2 heighfers 2 years old one white one sparked one aftar in the fforeheade: 7 yearelings oue black bull: one black heighfer with A white fface one brindled heighfer a white back: one brindles steare

memorandom that I Thomas minor of southertowne have fuly made over ale my lands at Tagwoncke as well that I bought of my son Clement as that which was given to me both upland and meadow with the Consent of my wife grace minor to my fouer younger sons Ephraim Josepth manaseth and samuell minor forever and to be Equaly divided between them: only Ephraim and Josepth are to have their share of upland lieing six score and fouerteen pole wide from the marked trees on the East side and the rest of the land westward to be manaseths and samuells the meadow to be as equally devided as they posiblely can Each one as much as another and Ephraim and Josepth to have the yuse of all the meadow from the time they go free from me till manaseth be of age p vided that they keep a Cow for manaseth and Two for samuell to the halfes that is to say to have the milke and halfe of the increase and if they put away the Cattell before then to give up their share of meadow when they part the Cattell or Els to hier it of them as they can agree with them: this witnesseth allso that Ephraim hereby is fully sattisfied both for what I gave him and what his Brother Thomas did give him of the farme I bought of Carie latham as allso Josepth This allso witnesseth that I have fully given to my son Ephraim the house at Tagwonke with the fenced lands as sattisfaction for the land Thomas gave him upon the farme that I bought of Carie latham this is the true agreement between al of us above mentioned as witnes my hand This .22. of June 1664   Thomas Minor

The .22. of september 1664. at a towne meeting There was acount given in of five pound five shillings and eight pence to be paid in mony .3 l of it was to be paid to deacon parke that mr noyce borrowed The rest was spent by sha and Elisha about the .5. of march for goeing downe about a minester as they say

The Choyce was made before: for goodman Chees-brough Chalenged mr stanton to make good his p mise to goe with him another owned it afterward and Aron fore-tould it 7 days

The 30th. of Januarie 1664 The Captaine Denison said that he was tould that our Towne bounds was to goe no farther then poquatuck River and this was the first time that I h(e)ard of it

The 13 of Januarie 1666 being sabath day I was at the meeting house and it was the Third sabath that mr noyce departed the meeting house and Taught at mr Richardsons

The Third of march I and my wife was at new london and mr noyce Taught it being sabath day

The 29. of march 1665. The Blacke mare had a stone Coult a Browne bay with a stare in the forehead thuse :} fouer blacke feet

The 26th of Aprile 1665 the whit faced young mare folled and had a bay stone Colt with a black mane & a blacke Tayl The 28 day marked it & a black mussel & black lips Emund ffanni(n)g had young daughter the same day

The bay mare of paines have a bay mare Coult with a blacke mane and Tayle The Roane mare have Red mare Coult with a Red mane a litell spot of white thus O: on the right side of the forehead ale fouer hoofes somewhat white the 19 day of may marked

About August the .22. 1667. The bay mare at mistick had a young Colt

monday & Tusday being the second and Third days of July 1666 Leeftenant James Averie & James morgan & we Ran the Townes bounds as ffolloweth
ffirst begining at the poynt of roks upon Captaine denysons land at misticke lying due Est from the sandie poynt of his land at mistick River we Ran six miles nor north Est to a Chestnut Tree at the midel of the uper pon(d) by lanthorne hill & formerly marked by Captaine denison Thomas minor & others

& from thence Two miles to an ashe Tree marked on
the north side of a litell brooke upon a north line
formerly marked by Capta denison Thomas Minor &
others by the Towne apoynted and from thence to a
white ocke marked with Ten noches which was our
north Corner upon a north line from the Eight mile
Tre Two mil(e)s That is Ten miles: from which we
Run seven miles upon an Est line to a white ocke
Tree and an half mile lieng to the south of a great
pond the Tree was marked fouer wayes and with 7
noches and a half more

This last will of mine is that if I never returne
from Bostowne That what ever is mine houses lands
moveables & unmoveables horses and Catele sheep or
whatever is mine I give to my loveing wife grace
minor to be hers so loung as shee liveth and at her
death to be disposed to our Children begoten by us
only this p vided that at the time yt paines mares be
parted I do give my sons manseth and samuell Each
of them a mare and my daughter hanah a mare then
to be delivered and my grant of 250. ackers of land
at the pou(d) to my son Clement: and at the dissase
of my wife the whole to be parted to our Children so
as to the younger ones manaset samuell hanah may
have their right and the rest equally to all John and

Clement overseers that this my will be p formed witness my hand this 21. of october 1667

Thomas minor

(This will cancelled in original.)

The .15 of november .1667. Ensing Tracie & Thomas lefingwell la(id) out one hundred and ffiftie ackers of land for me ling from the southermost End of the greate pon(d) To another pon(d) with all the meadow yt is on both sides of the River between the Two pons with a strip by the pon(d) so as to Joyne with the abovesaid Tracies and leafingwells land as allso all & Everie of the spots of meadow by the pon(d) so far as my land goeth a whit oak marked by the River yt coms from the 8 mile Tree belounging to stoneington an(d) in breadth fouer score pole or thereabout to a pon(d) on the side there of a mapell marked T M a forked mapell and in length To Tracies and leafingwells land a white oke marked at the brook side next mr Berewsters and another by the path that goeth to mr Brewsters by the pond End both Trees marked T M at Each end of the meadow as allso a greate whit oke by the pon(d) between the above said Two men an(d) me and Two ackers of meadow at a brooke called Ke-non-tu-tuck River. lying by a great Swamp with an whit oke at Each End of the meadow marked Thus T M by the upland

or upon the upland as allso one hundred ackers of
land about halfe a mile to The northward of stone-
ingtons corner Tree the length of it is halfe a mile
The breadth of it one hundred pole at the Corner
next to stoneingtons Corner a white oke marked Thus
T M ⚹ so the tree groweth the other at the same
End is a littell white oke marked T M the Tree
groweth thus ⚹ standing neare to a great Chestnut
Tree: from that in lengh to a black oke marked thus
T M and in breadth at the other End to a great whit
oke standing on the est side of a litell swamp marked
T M about 3 chaines from the Swamp

The .26. day of ffebruarie .1667. being wensday
we saw the Blase apeare in the skie neare To the
southwest or south west & be west it was verie loung
and sharp at the lower End

The .6. day of november .1668. we Eare marked
the mare Coult of the ba(y) mare and cut an halpenie
on the fforeside of Each Eare shee had a star on the
ffore heade

The .11. of may .1670 The Two mares folled the
14th. day we Eare marked the Coults the bay mare
have a bay mare Coult marked with a halpenie on the
fforeside of Each Eare shee have a white blase down
the fforehead and Two wal eyes my wives mare have

a bay horse Coult with a white blase downe the fforehead and a blacke mane and a blacke tayl ffouer white ffeet and an halpenie Cut on the fforeside of Each Eeare

The 28. day of Aprile .1672. the bay mare had a sorell horse Coult Eare marked the 29. day hee have a litle white snip on the uper Lipp the same day I turned out a black browne geldin he had a white face and fouer white feet: and A Redish gray geldin with a white face and A blacke gray geldin al three of them now a yeare ould and all three Eare marked with an halpenie of the fore side of Each Eare and branded with :K: on the neare shoulder and Γ on the neare buttucke and bay yeareling mare marked on the same as the other above mentioned and her mane black and turned to the left side and a bay horse of a yeare ould marked as the others the Two hinder feet white and a litle white streeke downe the face and a doct Tayle

and a sorell Mare of Hanahs a yeare ould with a white in the foreheade thus § and a browne mare of hers of a yeare ould with a litle white speck on the foreheade and both Eare marked and branded as the other above mentioned shee have a litle white speck on the uper Lipp:

The .9th. of may .1672. the white faced mare

that is Called my wifes had a bay horse Coult hee
have fouer black feet a blacke mane and a blacke
Tayle he have A star in the forehead: and the .10th.
day was Eare marked with an halpeny on the foreside
of Each Eare

The .23. day of May 1681 I begun with mr Leeds
to fferie us over

The 18 of march 1681–2 wee made even with
Leeds for my fferieing.

Mr pastor Noyse: mr stanton senior: I Thomas
wheeler Nathaniell Cheesbrough: Nehemiah palmer:
Thomas stanton Junior: Ephraim minor: moses
palmer: Tho: Minor begun the Church att stoneington in June 1674. the .7. of march .1675. goodwife
frink was admitted: The .14. of march 1675. mrs
stanton senior and Hanah minor Ephraims wife was
admitted The .11th. of April 1675. Joseph Minor and
his wife marie was admitted:: the .13. of June 1675
mrs Noyse was admited

This .24th. of Aprill .1669. I Thomas Minor am by
my acounts sixtie one yeares ould I was by the Towne
& this yeare Chosen to be a select man the Townes
Tresurer The Townes Recorder The brander of horses
by the generale Courte Recorded the head officer of
the Traine band by the same Courte one of the ffouer
that have the Charge of the milishcia of the whole

Countie and Chossen and sworne Commissinor and one to assist in keeping the Countie Courte

The .15th. of November .1674. Nathaniell Cheesbrough had six Children baptized and moses palmer was baptized and Ephraim Minors Daughters. Rebekah and Elizabeth was baptized: : the .13th of december we had the first sacrament: the 14 day the .2d. sacrament of baptisme was administred to Nemias Children and young Tho: stantons .8. Children: the .21. of march 1674 frinks .5. Children was baptized: : the .18. of April 1675. Joseph minor marie and mercie minor Joseph minor Children wer baptized

These may signifie to all such whome it may concerne that I haveing in an asembly of the Inhabitants of stoneington asked by goodman minors desier whether they as neighbours had ought against Thomas minor or his wife that they had not lived as Christians amoungest them and as such as were in Church ffellowship none objected against them

James Noyce

Stoneington July .14. 1669.

These are to signifie that all such whome it may concerne that we whose names are under written being members of the Church of Christe at new london doe owne Thomas minor of stoneington and his wife members with us and under our Care and watch and they do live ffor ought wee know or heare as doe become Christians

> James Averie
> william dougles

new london

> June .30. 1669
> In the name and with the
> Consent of the Chh

The Last day of november 1672 Clements wife was delivered of a daughter Ann and the .6. day of December shee departed this Life 1672.

The last will and Teastament of mee Tho: minor being in my perfit understanding and memorie it being the 72. yeares of my age June the .16. 1679 I doe ffirst bequeath my soule to god that gave it and my body to the grave untill the Resurrecktion: : and if I die before I doe make any other will: I doe ffrely give to my beloved wife grace minor all that is my owne moveables and unmoveables without Exception duering her life time to Dispose on for her Comfortable subsistance and after her death: if my soun samuell out live her to have and Injoy the houseing and the whole land that I bought of Carie Latham because hee have been carefull to uphold and Renew

the fencis at his owne Cost and been willing to carie
on the affaiers of the house in myne and his mothers
weaknes and I doe give and bequeath. all that of my
estate that shall be left at my wifes deseas to be
Equaly devided amoungst the rest of our Children
then Liveing namely John Clement Epraim Joseph
Manaseth and my Daughter Hanah Averie only one
Cow and one mare and one yew shepp to my grand
childe Anne minor now liveing with mee and my
wife: and thus I doe dispose of it in this maner because my deare Children have Everie one allRedy had
theyr portions according to my abillitie so praying to
god to preserve both mee and them to himself: I com-
mit all to him and rest in his mercie to mee and
them in Christ Jesus

Tho: Minor:
by me Canceled

The .16. of may .1683. John minor his children—

John Minor
Thomas Minor
Elizabeth Minor
Grace Minor
Joseph Minor
Ephraim Minor
Sarath Minor
Abigale Minor
Johanah Minor

Ephraim minor his Children

> Ephraim minor
> Thomas minor
> Hanah minor
> Rebekah minor
> Elizabeth minor
> Deborath minor
> Samuell minor
> James minor
> Grace minor
> John Minor

Clement minor his Children

> Joseph Minor
> Clement Minor
> William Minor
> Ann Minor
> phoebe Minor
> Marie Minor

Joseph minor his Children

> Joseph minor
> Marie minor
> Marcie minor
> Benjamin minor
> Sarah minor
> Joana minor
> Christopher minor
> prudence minor

Hanah Avery her Children

Tho Avery
Samuell Avery
Ephraim Avery
Hanah Avery

———

Manaseh minor his Children

Elnathan minor
Samuell minor
Hanah minor
Lidia minor
Thomas minor

———

(Worn   The .6. of May .1675. wee Turned   (Worn
off)   :Catle: and .17. horse finde .12. of   off.)
hanah .2. of Samuels

francis wheatherburne A
brot living with mr potter
(a)t Rappahanuck in virginea

The yeare 1661 my   (torn)
number I begun :so
so(lve) .48. years ould: which
were like to a bale that to
This yeare .1662. my selve I am
for to   evill is like me to ow (torn)
7 hom 1663

INDEX.

LIST OF INCOMPLETE NAMES.

PLACES.

BIRTHS.

DEATHS.

MARRIAGES.

VESSELS.

WILLS.

www.ingramcontent.com/pod-product-compliance
Lightning Source LLC
Chambersburg PA
CBHW030114030726
47498CB00007B/2377